To every person who lived through a traumatic injury to the body or to the Spirit and made the choice to move beyond their newfound limitations into their greatness unveiling previously undetected possibilities and talents,
and to every family member and friend who supported and continues to be there for those of us who choose to THRIVE! Don't Just Survive, I wish you countless blessings on your generous and powerful journey.

THRIVE!
DON'T JUST SURVIVE

ALI BIERMAN

Copyrighted © 2014 by Ali Bierman All rights reserved.

Purpose Publishing
Pp
Sharing health and happiness through edutainment

Second Edition June 2014
ISBN 13: 9780977316274
ISBN: 0977316270

This book was printed in the United States of America

DISCLAIMER AND TERMS OF USE AGREEMENT

(Please Read This Page Before Using This Book)

This information is for educational and informational purposes only. The content is not intended to be a substitute for any professional advice, diagnosis, or treatment.

The author and publisher of this book and the accompanying materials have used their best efforts in preparing this book.

The author and publisher make no representation or warranties with respect to the accuracy, applicability, fitness, or completeness of the contents of this book. The information contained in this book is strictly for educational purposes. Therefore, if you wish to apply ideas contained in this book, you are taking full responsibility for your actions.

The author and publisher do not warrant the performance, effectiveness or applicability of any sites listed or linked to in this book. All links are for information purposes only and are not warranted for content, accuracy or any other implied or explicit purpose. No part of this work may be copied, or changed into any format, or used in any way other than what is outlined within this book under any circumstances. You may use short quotes only in book reviews. Violators will be prosecuted.

Table of Contents

Introduction v
Acknowledgements vii
June 09, 1996, About 7:38 PM 1
The Aftermath 7
Emotions in Upheaval 17
The Brain Rehab Center 25
How My Life Came Together 33
Faith Kept Me Going – Still Does......................... 45
Hello Synchronicity 55
Powerful Thoughts 63
Deceptive Appearances.. 67
What I Discovered About Your Health 71
Everything Happens Perfectly Despite Appearances 93
CThe Second TBI 101
I Discovered True Happiness 109
My Inspiration 117
Loving Yourself First 121
Happiness or No Happiness: Choose 129
How To Make Your Best Decisions...................137
Afterword..141
Resources 143
How To Contact My Personal Healthcare Practitioners and Colleagues: 144
Bibliography 145
A Gift For My Readers 147
About Ali Bierman..149
Follow Ali: 150
Some Other Books You May Enjoy By Ali Bierman 151

Foreword

Every now and then on this life journey we are blessed to meet someone very special, someone that touches and impacts our life in magical ways. At the time we may not always understand these meetings, these divine intervened, possibly destined meetings. We just know somewhere at our core that we are in the presence of someone quite unique and quite special. I have learned to pay very close attention to such fortunate 'accidental' meetings. I have learned that they are never accidental and that I am about to be touched in some powerful, albeit subtle way. It is always, at least for me, one of those wow moments that I have learned to treasure. I have learned that there is no active preparation for these meetings. The preparation is merely being open and being present and letting the magic unfold as it will and as it is intended to. Please don't go looking for it, it does not show up in the looking for, or even the looking at, it simply shows up in the being...
It's not what you look at that matters, it's what you see...
Henry David Thoreau

And so as it was for me when I met Ali Bierman, I was approached by this slight, petite lovely lady at an event I was speaking at. She took my hand, introduced herself and touched my spirit with this amazing smile. You know the kind of smile I'm talking about, that smile that says I am really glad to meet and to know you, with no agenda or attachment. The smile that takes everything in and accepts it all and glows in appreciation for being alive on this planet. The smile, that simply wants to somehow hug humanity. By the way she later taught me how to really hug; now there is a rare gift.

Every person, no exceptions - not even babies – has something to teach and something to learn. Pay attention or you will miss the treasures life throws your way daily...
Ali Bierman

I have learned in life that there really are long dark tunnels that appear in our lives at times. And for some of us there is a spark of light at the end of that long dark tunnel. For others, who find themselves in such long and painfully dark tunnel's there is barely a flicker of light, barely the slightest hint of a light. That ever distant, ever faint flicker however was all that Ali needed. For her that ever faint flicker was the flicker of faith, of hope, of determination of sheer will. As you will learn in her story she would need every bit of that tiny flicker of hope and faith sparked by this great universe to begin a journey few will ever experience. Sometimes there is a tiny pull from somewhere in the vastness of the universe, a tiny whispered voice that calls to us. It's that pull and that whisper that gives us, when we pay attention, the strength to take the next step forward. Maybe it's barely an inch that we move, but movement forward is measured in the movement not in the distance. Ali is the example of how the spirit moves gracefully forward, attached to the movement, not attached to the distance and therein we traverse the vastness of the universe.

As a single footstep will not make a path on the earth, so a single thought will not make a pathway in the deep mind. To make a deep physical path we walk again and again. To make a deep mental path, we must think over and over the kind of thoughts we wish to dominate our lives.
          Henry David Thoreau

Ali Bierman ever so gently and not so gently at times takes us along with her on a journey through her tunnel through her mind. Her tunnel was created by a traumatic brain injury; her journey was guided by a flicker of universal light and powered by the spirit of a gentle yet determined spirit.

She openly, with great vulnerability, shares her emotions, her fears, her doubts and more importantly she tenderly and lovingly offers us a glimpse into the world of someone who has transcended the trauma of surviving a traumatic brain injury. In so doing Ali offers all those who have also suffered such a traumatic injury, a sense of hope. No, Ali offers more than hope; she rather serves an incredible example of 'possibility' and 'recovery' while examining the awesome re-creative energy of the universe. She redefines our common definition of bravery, or fearlessness and of abiding vision.

I am reminded of this piece of the great poem "The Road Not Taken" by Robert Frost...

I shall be telling this with a sigh
Somewhere ages and ages hence
Two roads diverged in a wood, and I
I took the one less traveled by
And that has made all the difference...

Ali Bierman did not listen to all the traditional medical notions of how her life was to be...

She traveled the road less traveled by and that has made all the difference, for her and for all of us lucky enough to know her.

Ali, I will forever be grateful that our two roads diverged in the woods of our life journey. Thank you for being you... You are touching lives... Your 'WHY'.....

By:
Frank A. White, MBA, PhD.
Frank White International
http://fawhiteandassociates.com

Introduction

The pages that follow detail my adventures through two traumatic brain injuries (TBIs) and my journey creating a new me – twice. People who knew me before my reinvention of me suggested I could inspire people by telling you *what happened* and *how I healed.*

When my Physical Therapist, Beth Richey, who helped me learn to walk again, suggested my quick healing might give hope to many people who feel discouraged by their life changes, and Heather Robinson, my speech/swallow therapist who helped me swallow and speak again, and my friend, Pamela Thompson also asked me to share my story, I decided to create this work.

Whether you or someone you love suffered a life-altering injury. I intend, within these pages, to let know you have a choice about healing. You can watch life go by and wish and hope for something to change OR you can learn how to recognize the healing cues coming at you daily, guiding you to discover your new direction in life. Please know that healing does not mean you return to your previous state. Healing is accepting yourself as you are now and moving forward as you re-invent yourself

I wish you love and countless blessings on your journey.

Ali Big

The Queen of Overcoming
Who Leaves You With a Song in Your Heart

Acknowledgements

Many people assisted me on my journey, and continue to offer me the support that propels me forward as I continue to re-invent myself each day. While that list is quite extensive I want to thank my physical therapist, Beth Richey, who asked me to write this book so that my experience might spur others on to create their own unique recoveries.

Pamela Thompson reiterated that suggestion and my speech/swallow therapist, Heather Robinson, made the third person asking me to share my story.

When the Universe sends me a message three times I know the message is more of a highly encouraged instruction than a coincidence. Having learned the importance of listening to and acting on the whispers (rather than waiting to get hit over the head with a two-by-four – as you will soon understand) of the Universe I produced the story you now hold in your hands.

Thank you to Reverend Jackie Holland who, upon learning about the tumor, told me, "Don't go through this alone." She accompanied me to the neurosurgeon visits and made sure I understood what was happening and helped me understand my choices. She also researched my neurosurgeon's reputation affording me the peace of mind necessary to undergo the surgery.

Crisis brings out the best in the people who support you while others simply disappear from your world. For me, the very best outcome of all these challenging moments is the fact that my brother, Ed, and I have become very close friends. He was the first person I called upon learning about the tumor. His communications with my neurosurgeon and his later help seeking solutions for me in the aftermath are priceless. I am so grateful he is a doctor with a knowing I lacked.

My daughter, Nili, became my biggest support immediately spreading the word through her network. She continually shared stories of people who survived similar surgeries – and their wonderful outcomes. She also talked with the neurosurgeon and my brother to really understand the situation and somehow knew how to help me through it.

Following the surgery, upon discovering the paralysis and its impact she again was out in her network looking for stories and surgeons who might ameliorate my situation. My brother continues in that role as well.

I am very grateful my daughter was able to fly in the day before the surgery and help me through all the paper signing and legal documents, and most importantly, held my hand the morning of the surgery. Also on that day, my dear friend, Reverend George Dashiell sat with my daughter sharing "the watch" with Reverend Jackie.

Crises bring families together. Thankfully my son, Damien, and my brother came into town following the surgery, loving me through the severe pain and terror of not being able to swallow, talk or breathe without difficulty.

Throughout those early critical days my friend, Stephanie Brooks Downing, stayed in contact with my daughter offering support and love.

I feel so much gratitude to my friends, Debra Temple and Elizabeth Richards, for being there for me when I finally made it home and my friend, Mary Garcia, who flew in from California to take care of me – and my home after Elizabeth returned to her family.

And then there was my dear faithful friend, Brett Nelson, whose daily visits and thoughtful treats of homemade smoothies helped me learn how to swallow again.

The Universe is as generous and loving as is the world in which I live. My spiritual cohorts from the Sacred Circle volunteered, under the direction and coordination of our warm loving leader, Jackie Luckenbach, to bring me food and provide transportation to doctor and therapy appointments until I was able to care for myself.

The injuries left me dependent on others and I want to acknowledge those who came through for me and made the difference I needed to move past survival to thrive.

My very dear friend, Peni Beattie, was totally there for me during my mom's final weeks. Sharing what she knew calmed my heart as I faced each painful moment of my mom's last weeks.

After the surgery, as more and more limitations and struggles revealed themselves, the Universe brought me caring friends who practice many healing arts. With deep gratitude for all your efforts and love, I thank Pamela Robinson, Specialized Kinesiologist, Dr. Rose Thomas, N.D., Dr. Scott, D.C., and Debbie Gibbons, Dr. Yvonne Fedewa, D.C., Wayne Faw for his guidance in health and introducing me to Dr. Todd Watts, D.C and Kinesiolgist , Judith Allen RN and Reiki Master, Ann and Gerry Hendrix, Mary Garcia, Elizabeth Richards, Debra Temple, and Stephanie Brooks Downing.

Please see the Resources page at the end of the book for contact information for each of them.

To my Virginia friends who called and sent love even when I was unable to talk with them – Dorothy Stone, Peni Beattie, Brooks McMullan, Marilyn Washington, Nusrat Zafar, Susan Neidethal, and Pamela Loughran. Whether or not we see each other I know you are always with me

Last but certainly not least, I thank all my readers and online followers who sent love, healing prayers and Light, as well as emails letting me know we truly are connected.

When I told my friend, Paula Heath, about my plan to launch my book, she immediately volunteered her expertise to assist that effort. Frank White, who honored me by writing the foreword, jumped in also helping me organize, plan and act as Master of Ceremonies for the event.

Blessings to each of you and a deep heart-felt thank you for being in my world and caring not just in word but in deed.

Persistence and consistency will get you every place you want to go in life.

Chapter One

June 09, 1996, About 7:38 PM

I remember feeling alarmed when I walked into the residential crisis care facility where I was about to start my night shift on June 9, 1996.

Why?

A young female arrived as a substitute for my male shift partner. The client who had attacked the copy machine just two days earlier was still in the house. I made the huge mistake of wondering how the night would go: calm or…

If you think something will hurt you it will. The power of the mind is everything. Putting emotions to your thoughts boosts their power and the speed at which you manifest whatever you focus on.

I unknowingly laid the groundwork for what was to come.

As I reviewed the status of the six current residents, the sun slowly slipped below the horizon. Being early June, the sky was not yet dark at 7:38 PM. Later I will tell you why the daylight matters.

Crash!!!

I bolted out of the office to find a mammoth of a person – the woman whose presence concerned me - throwing objects around the room. I ordered her into the office and told her to sit down in the chair just as I had done with her two days earlier.

Two days earlier she did what I said.

I assumed she did it this time too. To say I was surprised at what happened next would be a gross understatement.

I turned to talk with her, just as I had done two days earlier, in time to see her gargantuan hand about to smash into my left temple and jawbone.

She caught me off guard – not just because of the attack but also by the fact that her 419-pound body totally pinned me against the office furniture. I could not fall to the floor and crawl away. I could not scramble across the desktop. I barely had space to breathe.

I could not move any part of my body. I could not budge – at all.

Caught in a psychotic episode, she had no idea who I was or where we were. She continued to pummel my head – each time throwing a punch that jolted my entire body causing a nasty whiplash – a whiplash so severe my range of motion remained restricted for years.

Her size alone packed power in her punch. Her mental state – schizophrenic as well as developmentally challenged – magnified her strength. The psychotic episode boosted her already mighty wallop into an unfathomable force.

What Kept Me Alive

My thoughts split in two directions:

1. If I lose consciousness she will kill me and possibly ransack this entire facility, hurt the seven other people in this house and maybe then rip through the door and rampage toward the neighbor's house! 2. How can I escape?

Finally I noticed - when she pulled her arm back to power up her swing her whole body went back too on an angle that allowed just enough space for me to flit by.

I dashed out of the office into the open area with her in hot pursuit – clomp, clomp clomping after me. Thankfully she couldn't move very fast.

Her face, still contorted with anger, her eyes still ablaze with fury, she came after me flailing her arms at my head - again. But this time I could move. This time I could raise my arms and protect myself – which is precisely what I did.

Why I Stayed In Her Path

Remember the seven people in the house? I drew her toward me to keep her away from them.

A male resident witnessed the attack and told her to stop hitting me. My heart jumped into my throat as she turned toward him. I feared she would attack him. Surprisingly – she fell calm. The episode either ended or she had expended all of her energy. She stopped swinging.

The puzzled look in her eyes, that moments before revealed an altered mental state, faded now. It appeared the worst was over. I told the other residents to go their rooms. No way could this nearly quarter ton person make it up the steps. Heck, she couldn't even fit in the stairwell.

I told my partner to keep a close eye on her while I ran into the office and called the police.

Good Gracious. It took forty minutes for the police to arrive. Thankfully, during that time she did not go into another episode – well, not full-blown anyway. As my partner kept her confined to the kitchen that mentally ill person grabbed my partner's arm and bit it.

My partner wore layered clothing that night. The bite, thankfully, did not break her skin.

I knew we were out in the country, but it made no sense that it took forty minutes for the police to arrive. I cannot tell you I was relaxed while we waited – and waited – and waited "for the cavalry to arrive" - she said with just a tad of sarcasm.

I could not understand how the dispatcher failed to call this a dire emergency. She asked if the person was still on a rampage and when I replied, "Not this moment," she apparently chose to call it a non-emergency and notified officers to come out.

Seriously?

Finally, the squad car pulled into the driveway. Two strapping, tall, muscular officers walked into the office. Inside my being I felt the let down following a huge internal sigh of relief!!!

These physically fit policemen took one look at the attacker and called for backup, and backup and backup and for the patty wagon. They knew she would not fit in the back of the police car.

I had stood up to this 419-pound woman – developmentally challenged and schizophrenic in a psychotic episode – and I not only survived but also took control. Make no mistake; I know the Universe, coming to my aid, played a hand in the seeming calm.

Amazingly, when I took out her file folder to write the report for the commitment I found a completely filled out report written two days earlier during the day shift when she attacked the full-size copy machine, which stood *outside the locked staff office door.* Good thing no other residents had approached the office staff - *who remained safe on the other side of that locked door.*

[NOTE: Mental health workers get hurt and killed by the hundreds every year. I know because we treated some of them.]

This very woman had stabbed somebody in the face with a fork just two weeks before coming to our facility. I hope you're getting the idea that dangerous people walk amongst us.

While I wrote up the commitment papers, police officers continued to arrive until finally eleven strong officers stood in my office. They kept out of sight so as not to scare her. For her, being committed was a regular thing.

Does that fact tell you something about the state of the mental health system? There is more you need to know about the mental health system because I am pretty sure what I experienced was not, by any means, an isolated incident.[1]

When I went to the hospital for the commitment hearing I asked the security officer to protect me. He said, "Only the judge gets protection."

You might guess I was more than a bit nervous as I sat across the table from the attacker – easily within her reach. And with the security guard by the judge's side (not near me) I honestly did not feel safe.

But here is the point that really got me, really made me angry – the hospital psychologist served to make it clear to that woman that she had a choice: sign the papers agreeing to be hospitalized in the locked ward for a few days OR not sign the papers and be shipped off to the state mental health facility.

It was the job of the psychologist to make sure that woman understood her choices. Period. Nothing in the system protects the population at large from dangerous mentally ill people with the potential to inflict bodily harm.

But you already knew that, right? Look at the high rate of physical assault and homicide, at property damage – and the unthinkable.

Wait! It gets even better. The judge was the very same judge who, two weeks earlier, resided over the hearing after that woman stabbed someone in the face with a fork.

Yet there seemed to be no consequence for her to prevent any further attacks. Do you see a danger here? To you?

In that moment I learned that I wanted no part in such a system. Looking back I see the Universe had been trying hard to tell me that fact for

---

[1] To understand more about dangerous people in your everyday world I refer you to my book, *Mental Illness: Consequences When the Brain Misfires*. (See Resources at the end of this book.)

a while. Only back then, I didn't heed the whispers or even the gentle nudges. So the Universe shouted at me and took me out – because it was in my highest and best interest not just to leave that facility but also to leave the practice of talk therapy.

Seriously, your life and the lives of your family depend on you knowing how to protect yourself in this fast paced world of instant change and electronic information sharing.

Chapter Two

The Aftermath

We do what we have to do. On June 9, 1996, I stood my ground and I protected the residents in the facility – five foot three inch little me.

I didn't even know I was hurt. I didn't even think about it because I had a job to do. I finished my shift that night and filled in the day staff on the night's happenings the next morning.

When I went home I felt very shaken up yet numb. In fact, I felt numb, dazed, and confused. What had happened? I wondered, "What do I need to do for me now – right now?"

My neck and head were starting to hurt but the impact of the event had not hit me physically or emotionally – yet. Instinct told me to contact the therapist my husband and I were seeing for marital counseling.

Thanks to the Universe she was not only free and answered her phone but was free to see me right then. She told me to come see her immediately. She then called my husband to come get me and directed us to go to a medical facility.

When you get slammed and your brain gets hurt you do not think too clearly.

I felt very embarrassed that I had not been able to stop the event from happening. I didn't tell anyone what had happened for years – except my closest friends whose help I needed to recover.

I learned some interesting things about people and friends following that injury. People who I thought were my good friends, in some cases, fell out of my life. Others who I had not previously seen as particularly close became very important in my life.

That outcome puzzled me until I realized some people cannot deal with seeing someone they know in an altered state. My mind, body and functioning clearly had changed with no way to know how much I would recover of my previous way of life.

No blame - just a fact that had not occurred to me ever before in my life.

As I started on my journey, symptoms appeared slowly at first and then exploded. I think the Universe planted the small debilitating steps to help me cope with what was to come.

When you get hit in the head your brain sloshes across your skull to the other side. Yes, your brain is encased in a fluid sac to keep it safe. However, when your brain gets constantly knocked back and forth and back and forth it's going to swell and expand. Unfortunately, the skull is a confining space. Therefore, as the brain swells it bumps up against the bony ridges of the inside of your skull

The consequences?

Her repeated bashings injured my entire brain impacting every system in my body. It didn't take long for the pressure to produce a headache that made the migraines I endured for so many years seem like a walk in the park.

But the pain wasn't the worst thing to deal with.

My body and mind experienced unrivaled (for me) physical and emotional stress. Because of my background I knew I had developed Post Traumatic Stress Disorder (PTSD). I feared driving to the entire area of the county where my work had taken me – transporting clients to medical and psychiatric appointments.

I am talking about an expansive territory here!

People looked different to me now. I was on a constant vigil seeking signs of an impending attack. ARGH! I never felt that way before.

I desperately needed sleep to repair damaged cells and grow new ones to replace what I lost as well as to recoup the expended energy from the stress.

But every time I closed my eyes to sleep I saw bodies: strewn across a playground and airplanes flying overhead; there were bodies in some apartment in Manhattan; and atop a magnificent hand-carved Italian mahogany sculpture where a snow-white owl perched peacefully I saw an enormous snake slithering silently up to gulp the owl. "NO!" I opened my eyes in time to miss witnessing a horrible massacre.

Yes, it all happened in my imagination. Doesn't matter. When you dream you live the experience, don't you?

In all the nightmares (well, around-the-clock mares) I never saw blood. I never saw killing – just dead bodies and a planned attack.

There was no blood with my injury except inside my head. I definitely suffered a concussion. Closed head injuries (those with no open wound) are invisible. Consequently, nobody understands how hard someone with this type of injury must work just to get through each moment; after all, she looks fine.

A Saturday Night Live character played by Billy Crystal, whose famous line, "It is better to look good than to feel good," came to mind often in those days. I smiled to myself whenever I pictured that skit.

By the way, even though the performance was a satire – for the many who subscribe to that paradigm in real life I agree that one way to actually feel better is to work from the outside in. And then there are times when your healing must move from the inside out. Sometimes a combination of the two serves best.

Well, the symptom onslaught came on full force pretty quickly after that initial, "Let's get used to this whole idea" introduction. One of the first physical struggles came in not being able to maintain my balance with my eyes open – even when standing absolutely still. I was dizzy out the whazoo!

I saw the room move to the left. Then it stopped and started again – as if someone had made a video of my world and kept hitting replay: Move left. Stop. Resume previous location. Move left. Stop. Resume previous location. Truthfully that pattern continues today when I overdo or find myself in a busy environment.

ARGH! Often I just want to scream. But I don't because this part of my life has been around so many years I cope – not easily – but when I fall I usually fall against a wall or someone.

That severe dizziness caused me to lose weight during the initial week following the attack. DO NOT try this at home as a weight loss method. I in no way recommend that you get attacked and hit in the head to drop pounds!

I could not get up and walk the twelve or so steps around the corner from the living room couch into the kitchen and maintain standing long enough to grab food from the refrigerator and make myself a meal.

I have this bad habit of not asking for help. That behavior defined me then, and though I am way better at asking for help now, I continue to practice that behavior and the Universe continues to force me to create that new habit.

Because my functioning was so low I had to allow people to do things for me like prepare food and drive me to doctor appointments. Interesting isn't it, that the same need came up with the second brain injury? Well, of course it would since I have yet to learn and apply that behavior consistently.

So you know, I was embarking upon a lifestyle I never lived before.

And what I want you to know—most especially if you are a woman reading this book—is that it's not only okay to let other people help you with any tasks (big, little, or anything in between), it's actually wise and healthy for you to do so.

I will not dive into the brain chemistry to explain what's going on that causes you to feel you need to be Superwoman in this story. I certainly lived there for many years and this injury basically ended that modus operandi – well, temporarily. Still working at it.[2]

Think about how good you feel when you help somebody else. Give somebody else a chance to feel that good by helping you.[3]

Imagine—no actually you cannot possibly imagine this so I'll do my best to describe—how it feels to be in a world where four billion bits of information flash by every second stimulating all five senses. Well, okay, you live in that world. Fortunately for those of you with healthy brains, your filters work well so you never experience dealing with everything at once.

Before the attack, my brain worked to filter out all unimportant information about what I would see, hear, taste, touch and smell just as yours does now.

After the attack, my ability to screen out anything disappeared. Four billion bits of info per second and I took it all in on some level.

YIKES! I freaked out constantly!

Do you begin to understand the unfathomable exhaustion that overtakes people with brain injuries? Well, actually that is only one cause of the exhaustion.

What I finally noticed is that I ran my life making withdrawals from an energy bank account. We all do – it is just that we fail to see the incremental decline we incur by constantly withdrawing more than we put back.

---

[2] To understand and discover how to change the brain chemistry driving the super woman I recommend reading Dr. John Gray's book for the details, *The Mars and Venus Diet and Exercise Solution: Create the Brain Chemistry of Health, Happiness, and Lasting Romance* listed in the Resources.

[3] Learning how to receive will dramatically change your life as well as that of those who give to you. I made a video about The Law of Giving and The Law of Receiving. Watch the video here: http://howtobehappywithaib.com/give-receive

However, following a traumatic brain injury, a person has to use so very much extra energy in order to do the daily tasks of living that used to happen automatically and completely out of awareness.

The lives and functioning we take for granted. Oh wow! You have no idea how many tasks of daily life run on autopilot in every moment. Until you lose something you simply take it for granted.

It took a few months for me to realize that for every half hour of activity I did, I required two whole hours of just lying around in order to recoup enough energy for the next task.

I lived that way for three years. Hey. I was lucky (there is no such thing as luck – just an expression) that I got better in three years.

Of course, along the way I learned how to help others so that three years could be trimmed to one month for many people. For others, whose journeys do not include recovery of functioning or re-inventing oneself to thrive in an altered mind-body, that journey just goes on and on for a lifetime.

My next monumental struggle came from losing my short-term memory. I could not carry on a conversation. By the time you would get to the end of your sentence I would have lost what you said at the beginning.

I had to ask people to use very short sentences, and eventually at the rehab center, they gave me a notebook to carry with me. I learned to write notes as someone else talked to remind me what we were talking about! By then my hand had stopped shaking so I could write.

That situation left me unable to watch movies or listen to audio books. My favorite pastime activity was and still is playing educational material in the background at home or in the car. I learned an incredible amount of interesting info and skills by playing audios over and over.

Only, after the injury, I could not follow anything I listened to.

The attack happened one week before my final exams in my doctoral program. My study partner called me to ask a question. I opened the textbook and read a section aloud to her – but I had no clue what it meant. Before the attack I had all A's in my program and now I had no comprehension of the material.

Couple my inability to understand the material with severe exhaustion and you begin to see why I had to drop out of my doctoral program.

That choice devastated me. I was so sure I wanted to be a psychologist and now I saw no chance for that possibility. I felt as though my dream died along with so many brain cells in those few moments of the attack.

I knew all the information was somewhere inside my brain and I had no clue how to access it. Just finding words to speak became a chore. I still experience residuals in that area today.

My vocabulary was locked away, as if behind some secret door, along with all my psychology information. I could not find the key.

Before the injury I was pretty danged smart. I could excel at most anything: music, schoolwork, art, sports – you name it. People called me a Renaissance woman. I could even do home repairs.

After the injury I suddenly had dyslexia and ADD. I could not access my vocabulary or follow a conversation or the words in a book.

The injury tore me away from the world in which I lived, the life I knew.

One day a friend and I went into Washington. D.C. I wanted to show her one of my favorite museums.

I used to find my way by instinct. I just knew which way to go.

Being an avid fan of science news and documentaries I understood that some people are born with iron in their noses that acts as a natural compass. I only got lost one time in my entire life prior to the attack.

Well, that day I found myself totally confused. We went round and round in circles while I looked for familiar landmarks. I saw the sites but had no recollection of where the museum was in relation to those sites.

ARGH! I never felt so defeated. My kind friend agreed with me that we could visit that museum another day. (That event happened before cell phones and GPS systems came into existence). I was getting pretty dizzy and tired anyway.

When I got into the brain rehab program I usually got to the center easily. But I had lost my ability to reverse directions so going home often took me hours.

One day I found myself driving up and down the same street passing all the same neighborhoods. Looking at the map did not help as I could not interpret what I saw. Like my psychology textbooks, maps looked like Martian scratches with symbols I never saw before.

Suddenly I had major learning disabilities. Everything used to come so easily to me. New material usually came to me instantly. Now so much didn't make sense.

My arithmetic skills, and also my organizational skills, disappeared with the murdered brain cells.

Before the injury I knew, to the cent, the total cost of the groceries in my cart before going to the cash register. Don't ask me how I knew. I just did – regularly. That skill came in handy back in the days when I paid cash for everything.

Now I found myself unable to calculate the change due me on my bill. Unfortunately, that skill has not yet returned.

When I went to restaurants I had to ask my friends to tell me how much I owed including the tip. I could not even figure out how to determine fifteen to twenty percent of the bill to calculate the tip!!

Today I carry a calculator with me.

As for my organizational skills – now I have to screen out all other activities and focus intently on whatever project or papers I want to organize.

I can do it but organization is now an intentional effort for me – which means I expend great energy doing so. The good news is – I *can* do it.

One area I have not yet addressed is the vanity issue. While I may not be someone constantly checking out how I look in store windows and silverware, my appearance matters to me. My image and how I come across to others makes a difference in my life.

Until the injury limited by activity I kept myself in great physical shape and dressed well. People always guessed my age at ten to fifteen years younger than my chronological age. Frankly, I felt ten to fifteen years younger than my age in years too.

So it really threw me when I looked in the mirror and saw my hair had gone instantly gray. Yes, stress drains the color out of your hair.

My face looked haggard. I didn't recognize the person staring back at me from the mirror.

All of that self-reflection was re-enforced by one of the first doctors I saw in the original assessment of my status. For the first time in my life, the doctor wrote in my file, "46 year old woman who looks much older than her stated years."

Egad! His note really knocked me for a loop.

My mirror reflection was actually accurate and not simply my interpretation of what I saw.

Stay the course. The journey enriches you not reaching the destinatio

Chapter Three

Emotions in Upheaval

Lest you think I zipped into a Pollyanna world following the brain injury let me share what I was going through on an emotional level.

In the devastating aftermath of the injury – when I was in so much pain, when I was so exhausted, when my body needed rest but I couldn't sleep because of the PTSD and horrible death images I saw when I did close my eyes – mainstream medicine could not help me.

With all the hormone imbalances in my body, my brain functioning went whacko leaving me with suicidal feelings.

I literally talked myself into wanting to get through each day. I remember being very confused by the suicidal feelings. They made no sense to me.

Yes, this awful thing had happened and my body didn't work the way I wanted it to. I couldn't do the things I wanted to do. And because I had lost so many skills we take for granted, each moment of every day living had become a monumental struggle.

But that still doesn't explain why I felt suicidal. My emotions weren't making any sense to me – but that is still how I felt inside.

The psychiatrist I saw gave me one medication after the other as I repeatedly had an immediate negative reaction to each one.

I do not like pills. I do not take pills. My body-mind-spirit does not like me to take pills so I have reactions when I take most medication. And if I ever do wind up needing to take some kind of drug, I need a miniscule dose as opposed to what the average person takes.

The psychiatrist didn't believe I needed miniscule doses.

Why do so many doctors think they know more than we do about our own bodies?

And this doctor didn't know what to do when I had immediate reactions to each pill that he prescribed.

As a psychotherapist and a health fanatic I knew about psychiatric drugs and antidepressant in particular. Since my body systems were out of whack, so was my brain's ability to create serotonin and dopamine, the two neurotransmitters responsible for mood, motivation, focus – all the necessary elements of healthy functioning.

Without the ability to create my own serotonin to calm me and help me sleep, chances of licking the suicidal thoughts seemed hopeless.

Only I knew I didn't want to take drugs. And my body-mind-spirit made certain I would not fall victim, despite my circumstances, to the pharmaceutical industry and the unknowing doctors who support it.

Since low serotonin produces the symptoms patients describe when they feel depressed, big pharmacy created serotonin-producing drugs.

So patients get the double whammy of no longer being able to create healthy balanced brain naturally, plus they are subjected to a host of dangerous side effects.

The net result? Serotonin-producing drugs negatively impact brain health![4]

PLUS, since so many prescription drugs damage the liver, amino acids – vital to brain health – cannot be processed. Amino acids fuel the brain. High quality protein provides those amino acids.

I want you to know the whole picture of how serotonin drugs impact your brain's ability to reduce stress and thus impede calming you.

Under stress your adrenal glands release the hormone cortisol. Cortisol serves as Nature's protection allowing you to take action in a fight or flight situation. Of course in today's world that same sense of emergency may reflect the everyday pressures of life including money worries, being caught in traffic, feeling behind on a deadline at work or school, etc.

A body producing excessive cortisol begins to breakdown its own muscles (rendering it unable to build new ones), raises blood pressure, and causes weight gain.

What can you do then to counter the cortisol buildup that results from living a highly stressful life?

Learn how to meditate to lower your stress. Make a list of all that currently weighs heavily on your shoulders, causing you to lose sleep at night. Then take that list, examine it, and classify each entry as 1. Something you can control OR 2. Something you cannot control.

---

[4] For more information on the effects of cortisol on the brain and mental health:

http://bjp.rcpsych.org/content/180/2/99.full

http://www.huffingtonpost.com/sara-gottfried-md/cortisol_b_1589670.html

For those items on the first list write down a specific action you can take to eliminate that stressor and the date you will do so. For the items on list two simply let go.

So what did I do to keep myself safe and improve my mood?

Some years earlier I went to see one of the most gifted healers I ever met. At the time he helped me with a digestive upset.

I already knew that having letters after your name doesn't necessarily mean you are good at what you do. Think about the fact that fifty percent of doctors graduated in the bottom half of their class. Gotcha! Of course you have to be brilliant to get into medical school in the first place.

Avery Kanfer, known as the Dalai Lama from Brooklyn, is great at what he does and he has no letters after his name. While he is a psychic healer he doesn't just run energy but he also explains how you create your reality and how you create physical symptoms by what's going on in your emotional world.

When I initially met Avery Kanfer a few years before the trauma, he introduced me to the Seth book, channeled by Jane Robert, *The Nature of Personal Reality*. He told me I control my health and how I feel.

By recalling Avery's words I decided to no longer feel suicidal or depressed.

The instant mind shift caused an instant change in my body and brain that instantly ended the suicidal thoughts and the depressed feelings.

You might imagine, when I told the psychiatrist how I ended the unsafe thoughts and feelings he immediately responded, "That's impossible."

In his paradigm, changing your thoughts and changing your body-brain functioning by thought alone is impossible.

Where do you stand on the matter of choice and creating your reality through your thoughts and unconscious requests to the Universe (God, Source – whatever term feels right to you)?

Why would anyone buy into a debilitating belief system? Personally I refer to belief systems as BS.

Make sense?

Your belief systems do not come from you. They reflect programs entrenched deep in your subconscious mind from your early childhood, from people in your early environment. They set you up for the choices you make about what to believe and what not to believe. Thankfully, you can change those programs – with some help.

If instant change seems far-fetched to you, know that you can find documented cases of people with multiple personalities who broke out in hives or their skin revealed cigarette burns in one personality but not in another. Some people had diabetes in one personality but not in another![5]

The power of the mind to create your reality exceeds any force created by any human.

A Voluntary Trip To An MD

My physical health did a nosedive that first year following the injury. Again, I did something I just do not do – I went to see a doctor.

I chose a holistic doctor who immediately diagnosed dehydration. Of course the injury threw out my TMJ, which, among other things, increases the body's ability to hydrate itself.

---

[5] If you're interested in reading more about this phenomenon:
http://www.nytimes.com/1988/06/28/science/probing-the-enigma-of-multiple-personality.html
http://www.infinite-manifesting.org/MultiplePersonalities.html
http://www.scienceclarified.com/Ma-Mu/Multiple-Personality-Disorder.html

Plus, all the stress in my life had sucked me dry! So he gave me fluid intravenously.

The doctor also told me to eat animal protein. He said my health suffered because I lived as a vegetarian and my body didn't want me to avoid animal protein.

Whoa! Was he ever right. I do not like that animals die for me to eat. I don't even like that plants die to feed me. However, I saw a big improvement in my own health when I added animal protein back into my diet. In my case, eating meat and chicken gave my body exactly what it needed: the amino acids necessary to drive the process to create serotonin…naturally. Adding minerals my body craved – plus healthy exercise – allowed my body to start working again as it had previously had, and to heal my brain chemistry imbalances.[6]

Some people are not meant to exist on vegetarian diets. Very many people who think they are doing what is best for them by giving up animal products are slowly killing themselves. If you choose to avoid animals please educate yourself and test your blood chemistry to make sure it is the right choice for you.

Another myth emerging from the closet centers around the way grains impact the body and powerfully affect the brain. When I first stopped eating bread, fat dropped off my body and my energy level soared, allowing my recovery to take on new steam. As I removed all grains from my diet I discovered more clarity in my thinking and all around improved health and functioning.

Interestingly, the information now making its way into mainstream wellness has been around for decades. Like so many "not-the-usual" practices it remained suppressed by industries making big bucks off the myths.

---

[6] Please see Dr. John Gray's book, pages 174-175, listed in the bibliography.

I highly recommend reading the books written on this subject by cardiologist/best-selling author Dr. William Davis and renowned neurologist Dr. David Perlmutter.[7]

For those that believe in the scientific method, their works are filled with citations for research to back up everything they share.

Personally I recommend following your gut. When it feels good, do more of it. If it fails to bring you joy or peace stop doing it. You always have a choice. Some choices are more difficult to make than others.

---

[7] These books are listed in the bibliography.

Life is a do it yourself job BUT not a do it by yourself job.

Chapter Four

The Brain Rehab Center

I was so grateful when my nurse told me she had gotten me into the program at the only brain rehab center in the area. My first visit really threw me, though.

When I went to the brain rehab center the neuropsychiatrist who ran the place – you better be sitting down for this one as you won't believe it – recounted my recent life in a nutshell. He bluntly said, "You were a stay-at-home mom and you were safe. Then you decided to venture out into the world and you became a psychotherapist. And while you were out in the world you got attacked so the world isn't a safe for you."

He actually spoke those words to me!

Had I listened to him I think I'd still be lying around not functioning! Millions of people with injuries very similar to mine do. If I ever had any doubts about my need to leave talk therapy as a client or a therapist, they disappeared after this guy made his very judgmental evaluation.

To be clear, talk therapy does have its place. When you need a good listener (a skill far too many therapists never develop as they unwittingly push their methods and agendas on their clients) a friend simply cannot be the impartial listener who helps you sort out and then resolve your own issues. Plus, while sharing with friends is healthy and normal, dumping deep hurts may overwhelm them or leave them feeling helpless.

Thankfully, I never worked with the neuropsychiatrist who interviewed me. I found the rest of the staff there to be mostly helpful.

In the rehab center I developed a new look at life's priorities. I observed people whose injuries left them in worse shape than me.

The psychotherapist told me that people who came to the center following car accidents usually had no memory of the accident happening. The brain (well, The Universe) serves to protect them from reliving that horror.

Some people had no idea what they lost. I don't know if that is a blessing or not.

For me, I realized what I had lost. Before the injury I had a design business making jewelry, clocks and greeting cards. I played some musical instruments, composed music and sang my songs. I wrote books and was published in poetry collections as well as books by other authors, and in newsletters. Before the injury.

After the injury, because of the brain damage my hands shook so badly I couldn't hold the pen to write. I could not design or make jewelry and I could not play my music or write words. My shaking hands also prevented me from painting and my balance issue forced me to give up my regular exercise program at the gym.

I started writing at the age of six. Here I was unable to write. I discovered writing to be an addiction from which I suffered withdrawal!

All the methods I previously used to refuel my essence – my art, my workouts, my music – all of it fell out of my life.

No wonder my health began to crash. I felt totally crushed.

Oh, I got so excited the day I saw the Occupational Therapist (OT) for testing. Without my quick thinking ability her tests definitely challenged me. I thought, "Yes! Now they can see some of what I lost and finally I will get some help!"

Only that is not what happened. The OT told me my functioning met minimum requirements for daily life skills and they had no program to help me.

Okay, I feel very grateful I had not been hurt so badly I didn't know how to take care of myself. On the other hand, I felt terribly disappointed that no help was coming my way.

I knew from playing video games at home that using my mind and coordinating my hand-eye movement helped me heal. I also knew I became violently ill with a furious headache every time I sat at the computer since my eyes did not work right. Turns out my instincts were spot on, as my British friends say. Working my brain with video games spurred my healing.[8]

I was so hoping the center had something to work my eye-hand coordination, calm my shaking hands and challenge my mind and brain. Nope.

When I met one of the top OTs during my visit to New Zealand (actually we became very good friends and I spent three months in her house) I shared my OT experience. Knowing her reputation I figured if any program existed to benefit people like me surely she would know about it.

She told me the same thing the American OT did. My hopes went down the tubes.

ARGH! I experienced lots of ARGH moments following both brain traumas.

---

[8] After a severe brain injury nearly took her life, video game creator and enthusiast healed by creating a game to heal herself. Even if you never suffer a brain injury you can improve and extend your life while having fun in the process. Go here to discover how: http://janemcgonigal.com/

I saw people differently and often felt unsafe. Being out amongst vast stimulation I could not filter out sucked my energy driving me to nearly collapse – no matter where I was or what I was doing.

A very interesting thing happened. I am not sure if it relates to the disempowering thoughts of that neuropsychiatrist at the rehab center or where it came from, but somehow my car became a safe haven for me.

Regardless of how much my physical state spun out of control, just getting into my car and being still and silent (often I mediated) for 20 minutes revived me.

Somehow I created my car as a calming zone.

Sitting here thinking and wondering how or why I managed to accomplish that task the thought occurred to me that I bought that Volvo as a safe car - the one in which both of my kids became drivers.

Wow! I never made that connection until this moment.

No wonder that car became my safe haven. If I was out shopping and needed to recover my energy to make it through the store I would leave my shopping cart and go to my car and just *be*.

Sometimes I meditated and sometimes I just closed my eyes to shut out the world. There is no logical explanation for how I could recover just by being in my car. It is all about *what happened for me* – completely out of my awareness. My subconscious mind clearly ran a program that equated being in my car with peace, calm and safety.

Following the damage from the brain tumor surgery I find the same result. I always buy my cars by first checking the safety record. So when I retired my Volvo at 314,000 miles I bought a Subaru – the safest car out there.

It holds the same power for me. When I get overwhelmed (which happens when I am out and about and even at friends' homes) I go to my car and just rest until I feel okay.

Create a safe haven for yourself – some place you can go to calm down and recoup your energy. Note that I didn't have to drive anywhere. I just had to sit in my car – alone and quiet.

The Eye-Opening Lesson

I learned how so many millions of people live their lives every day – putting forth great effort to make it through what the rest of us call normal daily life experiences and tasks.

I never thought about what life was like for those who had trouble learning or didn't fit into the paradigm of learning still prevalent in most schools today.

I found myself seeing those I knew with learning disabilities and other physical disabilities too, as the true unsung heroes of society.

People called me an inspiration – because they knew where I had been, where I was after the injury, and where I was going. Yet what I accomplished paled in comparison to all those with invisible disabilities, many of them challenged from birth.

What a humbling experience for me, one for which I am eternally grateful.

That lesson moved me out of judgment and made me stop to think about how others see the world and the choices they make to get through each day.

Got A Question For You

When you need customer support and the agent is slow or doesn't understand your request – or if you are in a restaurant and the waitperson is slow or bumbling in some way – do you get angry about poor service? OR do you step back and ask yourself,

"I wonder what kind of day this person is having. How can I make it better?"

What do you think happens when you do the latter?

When I was in the brain rehab center I met a gentleman who was so incredibly proud of the floor he waxed and cared for in his church. This man, before his injury, had managed a crew of forty-three people at his job. Here he was, in his altered-brain life maintaining this one floor.

Oh my goodness! The lights came on for me!

He reminded me of one of the chronically mentally ill clients in the day center for the chronically mentally ill where I did my psychology internship. Jerry (not his real name) beamed with pride when he talked about how nice and clean he kept the car dealership where he was the janitor.

Those men prompt me to ask you, "Who would you rather see miss a day at your work place, the CEO of the company or the janitor who keeps the bathrooms clean and stocked, and removes the trash from your wastepaper basket daily?

Now, when I see someone cleaning up the restroom or stocking shelves in the store I thank him or her for doing such a great job. I let them know I appreciate them. I honesty do appreciate their work.

Recognition is a primary human need. Watch a face light up and posture straighten when you compliment someone doing a job that usually gets overlooked.

The brain injury tore me away from the world as I saw it and introduced me to the life I missed all those previous forty-six years.

How much richer I find each moment because of the injury that altered my brain and my functioning.

Please do not misinterpret my words. I know in my own functioning I go through periods when I feel exasperated at being unable to perform tasks that used to come easily to me – especially the fun tasks I enjoy like sports, gardening, painting, and playing music.

I *do* miss being the me I used to be sometimes; but mostly I prefer tackling this new task of reinventing myself as I am now.

Looking from the outside you may think I am nuts. I hope you never know how it feels being on the inside – unless it is your path in life to walk this way.

Everybody Sees A Different World

Funny, don't you think, we as humans think everybody sees the world the way we see it. We think everybody thinks like us and experiences events the way we do.

I was sixteen when I learned that not everyone composes music in their heads most of the time. Sixteen!

When one of my friends, who happened to be a psychologist, took me to a doctor's appointment following the injury she witnessed my need to stop while returning to her car. Right in the middle of a busy medical center I had to stop and curl up into a little ball to shut out stimulation and recoup enough energy to make it all the way to the car.

She asked what was wrong and I told her I was extremely dizzy and had to rest.

She struggles with anxiety and gets dizzy in high anxiety situations. She told me I was anxious and just to keep going.

Did her assessment of my status help me in that moment? What do you think?

Her remark took me aback. I didn't say anything. In my head I was thinking, "That is true for you not for me." She had not listened to me when I told her what I knew made me dizzy.

Later I found her remark did serve me, but not in the way she intended. She got me thinking about yet another gift of the injury –

I choose my thoughts and interpretations of life events. Everybody does.

One hundred other people make one hundred different interpretations of what I just witnessed and none of them match mine exactly.

Chapter Five

How My Life Came Together

The Universe gifted me very many eye opening experiences following that attack, which ironically left me with my eyes closed for a very long time.

Ah yes, the Universe works in mysterious ways. Letting go of understanding why things happen as they do, and instead focusing on what you can do now serves you and moves your life forward, yes?

When you live your life honoring the fact that each of us is both teacher and student and therefore the world is one infinitely huge learning circle then you enrich your life and the lives of everyone you meet.

Every person – with no exceptions, not even babies – has something to teach and something to learn. Pay attention or you will miss the treasures life throws your way daily.

Go back and re-read that last paragraph. You may not believe it.

Now, come along with me as I reveal how I not only survive but also thrive in a brain-altered body.

Going Within

When I was unable to follow a conversation I had to go within. The Universe gifted me with self-discovery.

I learned who I am and I learned about the Universe. Back then, it was just me, my Higher Self, and the Universe. Little outside of this made sense to me.

Somehow the Universe guided me to the work of Carolyn Myss. I don't know how it happened. I know synchronicity stepped in. Her work showed up in my hands. In particular, the first work was called *Why Some People Don't Heal And How They Can*.

Do you think the Universe gifted me precisely the subject I sought in that title? Of course. I applied what Carolyn Myss shared to move me into my own healing.

I played Carolyn Myss' tapes and videos over and over again until one day I started to comprehend her message. Then I continued to watch and learn. Each time I listened and watched, another wake-up call jumped out at me.

I was privileged to meet Bob Proctor shortly after the first traumatic brain injury (TBI). I took his original course, *The Science of Getting Rich*. Super course! I highly recommend it. Seventeen years later, I listen to, study, and teach the lessons.

I recall hearing Bob Proctor explain that when you see or hear something new when reviewing a book or video, "It's not something that wasn't there before. It's something in you that wasn't there before."

In other words, you only see what you are ready to handle.

Oh goodness! That truth shows up as a cornerstone in every piece I write and every session I do with every client.

David Nagel taught the weekly sessions for *The Science of Getting Rich Course*. Maybe you heard of him. He is one of the top names in the self-development industry.

David changed my life. I was angry with him for years until I understood how he helped me.

I told David my head was in so much pain I could not focus on the teachings of the course. He told me I chose to feel that way.

It didn't matter that I had been through a physical attack. David told me I had a choice about how to respond and go on with my life.

Years later when I figured out his lesson I thanked him for the words I will always remember. Perhaps that day marked the first time I heard the message of creating your reality as a series of choices you make yourself.

Hmm. Maybe that statement is not exactly accurate. David framed the truth in a different way for me. Looking back at my life I see my family actually taught me the same concept years before it became a buzzword.

You see, after my dad left home and then left this lifetime at the young age of forty-five for him and eight for me, my mom worked all the time to support my brother, myself, and her own mother.

Fortunately, my Bubby (my Jewish grandma) came to live with us whenever the weather was warm. She had a lot to do with how I grew up.

When I was in my sophomore year of college I contracted such severe bronchitis I had to drop out of school. I remember my doctor didn't recognize me because I looked so bad. (That was back in my pre-health fanatic days).

I was so sick. It didn't matter, though. I was so stuck in feeling so sick! My Bubby told me to get out of bed and get on with my life. Her exact words were, "Get to yourself."

My Bubby lived in much pain every day but never ever complained. She took care of us, she took care of the house, and did all she could possibly do given her physical challenges. And my mom never complained about working so hard either.

Great role models – the best, actually. They did everything out of love. Only they too did not do much just for themselves. That is one family tradition I am very grateful my daughter finally ended.

Looking back I see they made choices every day to make the best of the situation regardless of what it took.

You know what? Today, because I know my mom and Bubby come when I call them, I still get that strong message and loving support from them via their energy.

That is a story for another time and some of my other books.

Carolyn Myss' work, *Energy Anatomy*, brought me back into the world, set me on my path to healing and launched me on my career path as a Specialized Kinesiologist.

Energy Anatomy reinforced what I learned from Avery Kanfer. Avery taught me that I create my reality and that emotional issues manifest in the body as physical conditions or vulnerabilities – as did Carolyn Myss.

You may be wondering about the concept of emotional issues. An unexpected attack isn't an emotional issue.

An attack is a situation that I allowed myself to draw to me by not acting on what I knew to do for myself, i.e. leave that job and facility. So I became vulnerable to certain types of injury because of what was going on in my own life. Specifically, as you will learn in the chapter about the brain tumor, I was not doing what I came here to do in this lifetime!

Discovering the information in all the works I was slowly beginning to digest did not make me instantly better.

Remember, my body and mind were in a "bad way."

There I was: dizzy out the whazoo, unable to use my eyes without great distress and pain, unable to follow conversations or entertainment, experiencing physical issues that included severely unbalanced hormones and so much bleeding I had to get IVs to replace lost fluids more than once…and more.

Now where is the gift in that situation? How did I even know to look for the up side in all that down side?

I thank Carolyn Myss for presenting the notion that our

emotional baggage creates poor health.

I didn't have the language at the time. I had no clue about the law of attraction or the fact that whatever you focus on expands.

What I found is that my world showed up as I thought it would. To put it another way, my expectations always came to fruition. If I expected good then I saw good. If I expected disappointment – well, that showed up as reliably as had the good.

You see with your brain not with your eyes. Your brain does what you tell it to do! I didn't know that, did you?

To make certain I would go within and discover the True Me, the visual distortion I experienced with my eyes open was so severe that I could not stand still without losing my balance. I made an empirical decision – well I felt that choice was forced upon me actually – to keep my eyes closed as much as possible until (and when and if) the status of my vision changed.

After the brain injury had me seeing walls that wiggled and buildings I knew were not the shape I was seeing, I discovered the brain interprets incoming light. Your eyes do not see. Your brain sees. And my brain, which was most definitely not working the way it used to, saw amazing things.

The good news?

After energy work by Carl Ferrari, D.C., restored my visual center to normal, I realized with my new knowledge of how my eyes and brain worked that I could play games to amuse myself – with nothing more than my eyes and something to look at.

Exercise Your Brain

I still play with my vision/brain and making stationary things move. I enjoy watching two-dimensional objects appear 3D. Hey, I can generate FUN if I ever find myself waiting some place with nothing to read – simply by finding a pattern and moving it about, very much like viewing 3D pictures.

I LOVE 3D pictures! I have lots of 3D books and I highly recommend getting some yourself. You can control whether you see the 3D effect coming forward or retreating backward leaving a "hole" where the moved object actually sits.

What a great brain game!

Most mornings, before getting out of bed I enjoy making the fan above my bed disappear. And so it does disappear from my vision. Let me explain since I am not doing magic – just seeing the world as it really is rather than how it appears to be.

Do you remember studying about atoms and molecules when you were a kid in school? Maybe you remember that physicists describe atoms as mostly space with electrons and other subatomic matter flitting in and out of existence.

When I make the fan and entire light fixture disappear I am really seeing the space between the atoms that compose the molecules that make the fixture appear to be solid.

Does the light/fan go away? Hmm. Quantum physics tells me it ceases to exist. But you probably think it is still there. You'd likely see it – but I don't.

What's the upshot of all this experience and sharing? I know what Einstein said is true (okay, he spoke LOTS of metaphysical realities): "Reality is an illusion, albeit a persistent one."

When people tell you to exercise your brain they usually refer to brain workouts. Yes, those activities help keep your brain working well. However, an even more impactful workout involves the physical workout. Move your body to build and maintain a healthy brain and overall health.

A Word About Bumping Your Head

Whenever a person bumps his or her head, consider checking for normal functioning. What appears to be a relatively minor bump may hide damage within.

The bicycle accident in your early years may have gone unnoticed yet the possibility of slight damage building over decades exists.

Even if no symptoms show or the symptoms disappear in a short time, realize there is a high probability that damage continuing inside the brain becomes more and more prominent revealing more and more symptoms as time progresses.

Some dementia "victims" forget about the fall when they hit their head thirty years ago – because a lack of wound prompted no response in a medical or even a non-medical way.

Scary, huh?

If you or someone you know survived a traumatic brain injury *know* this fact: all brain injuries are traumatic. Just as you can't be a little bit pregnant you can't have a minor brain injury.

In my experience, a Specialized Kinesiologist who knows how to check your brain (no MRIs, no medical tests) can let you know if everything is okay.

When I saw Carl Ferrari, D.C., he confirmed I had lost consciousness – momentarily. I was not even aware that I had missed a moment since I was so focused on the event during the attack. Knowing what he discovered helped him restore healthy functioning to my brain. Thank goodness.

Always seek help for a brain injury but not necessarily from the neurosurgeon who treated you. His or her job is to clean up your brain and keep you physically alive – not tend to your quality of life. That job belongs to a host of rehab therapists.

Not only could I not filter out everything that I could see and hear but my hearing became supersensitive. I experienced every sound magnified at least ten times. I could hear things going on a block away.

Sounds were excruciatingly painful to me and my family got very upset when I asked them not to play the radio. I couldn't deal with the noise and they didn't understand why.

Fortunately for me the Universe directed me to Carl Ferrari, D.C., the creator of Neural Organization Technique (NOT). In a matter of minutes he restored my hearing to the normal range leaving me only the challenge of seeing.

In a later class he corrected my vision by working on the visual center of my brain.

Oh! I will share this critical (to how I work) piece of information now.

Dr. Ferrari had to heal my vision center two times. Why?

At the beginning of my saga I told you the time of the attack and the fact that 7:38 PM on June 9, 1996 was dusk not dark in Northern Virginia.

From Dr. Ferrari I learned that our bodies are the most powerful computers on the planet storing every event in great detail. Your super power computer records the lighting, whether your eyes were open or closed – and even the weather conditions, as the event happens.

Originally I told Dr. Ferrari the attack happened when it was dark outside and the lights were on inside the office. So he did his work replicating those conditions in my body.

Six weeks later, much to my dismay and disappointment, the vision problems returned. I didn't know why until the following year.

I happened to be looking out the window about the same time of day the following year. Wow! I noticed the sky was still light because it was dusk – not dark.

When Dr. Ferrari programmed dusk into my body and repeated the same energy work, my eyes got better and stayed better.

Remember, it was not my eyes but my brain that was off. My brain sent inaccurate messages to my eyes telling them how to move. My brain also misinterpreted the information my eyes fed into my brain.

Dr. Ferrari became my mentor and also a source of hope for healing.

Muscle Memory and Healing

This next experience gives me reason to believe I can heal despite severed nerves in my brain.

Muscle memory and cell memory hold steadfast. That fact allows incredible healings – the kind so many people (especially many medical personnel) call impossible!

I know someone who reads these words will get help as a result of my sharing the truth of muscle memory as I personally witnessed it.

Dr. Carl Ferrari seemed to perform magic for countless people, including me. We learned his technique of Neural Organization Technique (NOT) with hands on experience and live demos so we knew exactly how to apply his method.

One afternoon a young woman wheeled herself into the room using only her left arm and leg to move.

Ten years earlier a stroke left her right arm and leg paralyzed.

The first thing Dr. Ferrari did was ask her the date of the stroke. You don't forget things like that (witness my recalling the time of the attack way back in 1996). She told him the stroke and paralysis happened on February 22, 1989. (I'm making up a date as the actual one does not matter.) He did some quick muscle checking to see her current limitations and abilities.

Dr. Ferrari then told her body that the current date was February 21, 1989. He repeated the same evaluation – with startling results: the previously paralyzed muscles responded healthfully and normally, i.e., full functioning – no paralysis.

He explained that her body still had muscle memory of how to function and went on to do NOT. In less than forty minutes that woman had resumed full use of her right arm and leg. Dr. Ferrari told her to stop using the wheelchair and throw away the sling that held her arm still all those years.

I saw the whole thing with my own eyes. Frankly, that moment keeps me motivated in my own healing today. Unfortunately Dr. Ferrari left this plane some years back so I cannot experience his magic directly from him.

I figure if she healed, and in a matter of minutes, then I can too. And you can too if your journey includes recovery of functioning or mindset adjustment to accept yourself as you are now.

My intention here is to let you know to *never give up*. Nothing is impossible unless *you* believe it is impossible.

I wrote this book because so very many people (including my rehab physical therapist) urged me to share my experiences, especially my initial fast return of functioning while my body continues the deeper work out of awareness to others. For me, my continued healing remains very much an on-going process in my awareness. Take my word for it, life looks easier than how I experience it. And that fact happens for most, if not all, people with invisible injuries.

I wrote this book to serve as a healing agent, not a pity me tome. Congratulations for sticking with me so far. And if you are reading this work to help someone you love – what a priceless gift you bestow. Many blessings your way.

Of the many lessons I learned in this seeming tragedy, one of the biggest is that everything happens for a beautiful and Divine reason. Everything happens perfectly. Even the most horrific circumstance serves your highest good.

Phew! That lesson does not come easily to anyone. Yet if you look across the lives of very successful people you often find a traumatic experience that changed their lives – something they refer to as the greatest gift of their lives.

The gifts of this injury quickly became apparent to me. When I shared my discovery with the psychotherapist in the brain rehab center he told me that the only time he saw people heal from brain injuries was when they found the gifts in the situation.

Gifts?

When you look for the gift in a situation you will find it – guaranteed. The greatest gifts of all often come disguised as severe pain and suffering.

Think about the fact that the Japanese language has a single word for challenge and opportunity. Do you see the lesson yet?

I could have chosen to give up on life after the severe pain, limitations and suffering of the first TBI. So very many people do give in to a life of – well, watching life go by rather than doing whatever it takes to participate.

Taking every bit of energy you can muster simply to be present in a situation demands a strong and consistent desire to move forward. Not everyone is up for that task.

Yet everyone has that choice.

Everything in life is a choice. Some choices are more difficult to make than others. Trust me on that one! I live that truth every single day.

Healing Is Always and All Ways Possible

I want to encourage and support people in knowing that healing is always possible, regardless of circumstances.

Oh, I hear a backlash from that sentence!

Something I learned early on in the injury – knowing all I had lost (the seriously deep hurt comes from knowing what you lost) is that healing does NOT mean returning to your previous state. Healing means accepting yourself as you are now – altered mind and body – and going forward from where you are now.

I call it re-inventing myself and I have been through this major life overhaul twice.

Actually, I am still redesigning my life and still in the healing stage of the second traumatic brain injury. In the process – not done yet – but baby, look how far I've come.

Chapter Six

Faith Kept Me Going – Still Does

Ah, little did I know the extraordinary plans the Universe had in store for me. Somehow I knew the Universe held me with Love in Light – just as it does you in every moment.

I just needed to never give in to what others saw as hopeless or too hard a struggle to endure.

I refer to the four million plus survivors of TBIs who mostly watch life pass them by because, more than likely, someone with letters after his or her name wearing a white coat, said, "This is as good as it gets. Learn to live with it."

Of course the huge problem lies in the fact that many doctors live in specific paradigms. Most only know how to treat symptoms and have no interest or education in looking for the causes.

For many doctors with inflated egos, when the tests they know show no results they tend to tell the patient, most especially female patients, there is nothing wrong. They say the problem is in their head and they should go talk to a psychotherapist.

I know. I saw one doctor like that. He had no clue what test to run that would reveal the injury site. So he arrogantly told me there was nothing wrong. He was an eye specialist whose appointment waiting list stretched out for three months.

The fact is my problem was hugely in my eyes not working right. But his tests did not see the problem at all.

Thankfully, my persistence led me – finally, after three years – to the doctor who knew which test should have been performed three years earlier, given my symptoms. Sure enough, this new doctor's test results showed exactly the damage that led to the suffering I had endured.

I am grateful too that his test results also led to the kind of therapy that was designed to treat that issue.

Interesting? Very sad and terribly frustrating, in my humble opinion, that I suffered for three years because the first doctor could not admit he had no idea what was wrong or how to help me.

Think about how many people give up on resuming a normal life because of words like that coming from someone with *seeming* (heavy emphasis on the word *seeming*) credibility.

Choose to base your choices in healthcare – and everywhere else in life – on results achieved in true practice.

Now that is one message I find very important to share.

Oh yes, lest you think I do not like doctors, know that I am completely aware a neurosurgeon removed that tumor – an M.D.

As for letters and degrees, did you ever stop to notice and put together the fact that people create classes – and people create degrees and people create associations – so others think they get value in having those letters after their names or certificates on their walls stating they are a graduate of such and such?

Hey, I know. I teach classes myself for which I award certificates to those who want one. I know what I teach is life changing. I also know many classes out there only serve to make money for the teachers. Think coaching academies that "certify" graduates. The student pays to participate. Whether or not they have a clue how to help people, in far too many cases, that area remains dubious since only a few programs set standards or tests to pass.

Not all programs are scams. But beware where you put your money and your time and your effort.

Personally, in my own certification class, people do hands on work so I make sure they do the processes accurately. Too often that is not the case.

For example, as I shared about how I change the way I run my head (i.e., thinking) to make my highly challenged life workable, one life coach said it was all well and good that I could do it but she could not. She went on to say not everyone can change their thoughts and change their lives.

Is that not the point of most of the mindset books, courses and teaching out there? Doesn't quantum physics prove that reality?

Can a person lead a new and different life without making any changes? Can you change anything without changing your thoughts first and actions second?

Choose to live with awareness. When you decide to get better, whatever get better means to you, find someone who already did what you want to do, not someone who desires or read *about* doing what you want to do with your life. Only someone who lived through a similar experience can truly assist your life change.

You are an individual and no matter how much your injury looks like injuries suffered by others, your uniqueness determines what will work best for you. As in business, a guru may share his step-by-step trail to his success. But you are not him. You will not bring to each step the same stuff he did.

When your world crumbles following a life altering injury, you seek help in creating your new way of being in the world. Never mind the trauma. If your life does not look the way you think it should by now, why not seek assistance?

I personally believe no person is meant to go it alone. I also believe every person who accomplishes something significant in any area of life works with a coach or mentor – whether live or via a person's work.

Work With a Coach However that Looks For You

Carolyn Myss served as my mentor when I lost my short-term memory in the brain damage following the attack. Though I never met her in person (but did exchange snail mails), her work done back in the 1990s, helped me awaken to how the mind and body work.

Her teachings (through video, audio, books and PBS specials) led me out of my own dark tunnel into the light that allows me to help so many people in a way I never knew existed back before the injury.

If you think I harp on this message you are right: everything happens for a beautiful and Divine reason. When you look for the gift in the pain you will find it. *You will only find it when you look for it.*

Healthcare With and Without Caring

Let me give you some background as to why I received, theoretically, the best care available in the wealthy county where I worked.

The small staff in the facility was already one short due to a firing and the county refusing to hire a new person in the position. Cutbacks were happening back then. Not replacing the fired person meant no one lost his or her job.

The county wanted me back on the job ASAP. To further that effort, and since I had filed my case with Worker's Compensation, the effort to get me well included a nurse, hired by the county, to handle my case. She got me in to see all kinds of doctors and specialists. I am talking about specialists (like the one previously described) who had waiting lists three months long.

I got in right away.

In total, including the staff at the brain rehab center, sixteen healthcare practitioners worked with me. And that number does not include the additional specialized kinesiologists and energy workers who treated me – successfully, I must add – at my own expense.

The mainstream medicine doctors split into two camps: those who told me there was nothing wrong and it was all in my head (to which my response was of course! My brain is in my head), and those who said they could not help me.

That first group included doctors who had no clue how to proceed, who did not know which test to run other than their usual battery, which showed nothing in my case.

The other group told me that healing was not possible for my kind of injury.

Please get this message: just because a doctor doesn't know what to do and is not willing to step out of his or her box to investigate new possibilities in no way means nothing is wrong OR that no means to improve your life exists!

Never let anyone bully you or deny your suffering. Push until you find the doctor who does know how to help you – no matter how long it takes. And never buy into the paradigm of a doctor who acts like he knows everything and tells you either nothing is wrong or you will not get better. That is his or her belief system – what I call his or her BS.

Refuse to buy into the BS of a doctor who clearly displays his arrogance and self-centeredness and thoughts of superiority. You know that guy: he is a legend in his own mind.

You get to choose to ignore their paradigms instead of letting them take away your hope. There's always another way to look at things and a different paradigm for you to jump into.

I remember the day the doctor in charge of my case told me, "This is as good as it gets. Learn to live with it." Well I knew how much I struggled to get through each day and I wasn't willing to accept his verdict because that's what it was actually: a life sentence.

Who made him judge or, in this case dashing all hope, who made him God? How dare he make a statement to take away my hope!

The truth was and is that he had no clue how to help me heal. The impossibility of healing was *his own* BS.

What really vexes me is that those words are spoken to people every single day (probably lots of people every single day) by doctors who don't think outside the box and are therefore limited by what they know, and think what they know is all there is to know.

If I sound angry it's because I am. Why? Because I see so many people whose hopes were dashed by words of a doctor who says impossible means impossible.

The day those words fell on my ears I took two actions: First, I told myself I do not live in his paradigm. I will get better. Next, I wrote a song about the gifts in every moment and the gold-lined path I follow every day.[9]

When I started my healthcare practice, I did it because I didn't ever want anybody to give up because some doctor, who they likely saw as a God, spoke that hope-killing pronouncement.

For many years I told people, "If the doctor says I can't help you I probably can." I do before and after checks in the session to

---

[9] You can listen to my song, *Still Becoming*, to discover my healing magic at http://howtobehappywithalib.com/becoming

get clear before and after status evaluations. And in pretty much every case the people who came to see me did improve.

No, they did not completely heal in one session. I created a series of sessions – we're talking three maybe four sessions – that help people achieve extraordinary health, emotional, physical and spiritual.

Just know there are many ways to heal and if I had listened to that doctor and if I had given up all hope, I don't think I'd be alive today. Every day living was just too hard.

When I came to the revelation that the Universe hit me upside the head with a two by four disguised as a 419-pound mentally ill woman, I easily saw the gift it gave me of allowing me to heal myself and to make the bold statement which I advertised for so long.

I made a decision to never ever leave anyone without hope because a doctor pronounced him or her limited and hurting for life. In fact, I set myself a goal of reaching three million people with my message, impacting every life for the better.

Now that can only happen through my writing and online work, videos, coaching, etc. – all the ways I spread my message and meet with people across the globe.

The many modalities I learned served me and served others whom I could help. Not all of them worked for me. I only delved into those that made an immediate difference for me. Then I combined everything I knew into my own unique way of working.

In my own mind and experience, healing agents work that way. They take what they know and create their own way of working – that works.

This may sound woo-woo when I share that every powerful healing person I know channels through the healing from the Universe. However, I do not know anyone who actually helps people energetically who doesn't channel Divine guidance.

You know, this information is not really woo-woo at all. For me, when someone I know is ill or facing surgery I do not just pray for them. I also pray for the medical team caring for them.

Come to think of it, one of the greatest gifts of the brain injury following brain surgery (I will get to that one soon) was my recognizing the messages that come to us non-stop every day, showing us how to lead the life we want to live.

Everyone receives those messages. The thing is most people are unaware the Universe communicates with them all the time and they have no idea how to receive the incoming message OR how to speak directly to their own Spirit and the Universe.

Quick example: one night en route to a party, I missed my turn as directed by my GPS. The street was so dark I could not see any street signs. I drove up and down the main road trying to read the street signs.

Not possible.

So I asked the Universe to take me to the place. I went directly to the place – no wrong turns. Actually that happens for me often. I do better trusting guidance than using the GPS.

I trust the Universe to guide me through my life every day too. I am certain the Universe responds with synchronistic events upon which I act. No brainer! When I fail to take the actions my spirit nudges me to take, I always regret my choice. Know what I mean?

I learned only to work with people who really want to change. Know why? Change happens instantly. What takes so long, maybe a lifetime and maybe never, is getting *ready* to change.

If anyone tells you *they* can heal you, I advise you to run as fast as you can in the other direction. No one can possibly heal another person.

Huh?

First, the person has to want to heal. On very rare occasions I worked on clients who said my work made no difference for them.

My before and after evaluations proved otherwise. Yet, despite the fact that anybody else present could see the difference, they insisted nothing had worked.

Those individuals had invested in not being well. Very many people identify themselves by their ailments or issues – emotional or physical. Without that label to hide behind, they do not know how to be in the world.

Fact.

Again, I want to remind you that healing does not mean returning to how you used to be. Healing is accepting yourself as you are now and moving forward from here.

I recall sitting on my living room couch one day, before the pronouncement from that doctor, wondering how to live my life if I never got better. I asked if the point of the pain and loss served as a stepping point to something new and totally unknown to me.

No, I didn't listen for voices or see visions. Interestingly, I got the message I was to be an inspiration. Before long people started telling how much I inspired them. Interesting, huh? But I then replied, "I made a choice to act regardless of circumstances rather than sit back and watch life go by."

In my own mind there was nothing inspirational about my life. For me, I simply made self-empowering choices. Besides, I knew that one's actions speak more powerfully than words ever could. People do what you do not what you say.

Be the person you want others to emulate. In your becoming you, you promote healing for all.

Do you realize that every day the Universe asks what it can do for you? If not then you allow your requests to go out unconsciously so you keep getting what you don't want.

Chapter Seven

Hello Synchronicity

The Universe, as it always does, quickly came back to me with a response to my pondering. Synchronicity came into my awareness.

At the time of the injury I worked with a massage therapist. He had moved into a healing center with many different modality practitioners.

There I met someone who showed me an experience with magnets. Wow! In one of the online support groups I found for TBI survivors and their families, I had read about how magnets help the brain heal.

No coincidence that my masseur introduced me to the person with the magnets – in particular, the magnetic sleep system which ultimately restored my life to normal.

AND, in that same healing center I found my first Reiki master who relieved my eye pain instantly – though not permanently.

Wowsers! Now I understood something about the energy of the Universe. Now I had a sort of explanation for what happened when I put my hand on my daughter's frequent dance injury areas and we both felt heat which led to healing.

Soon I became a Reiki Master and witnessed what others would call super natural events when I "ran energy" on them.

Ah, synchronicity.

Through the connections I was now making in the energy practitioner world I found Fred Gallo, PhD. I studied his Energy Diagnostics and Treatment course (Energy DX & Tx). Dr. Gallo took Dr. Roger Callahan's Thought Field Therapy to a deeper level.

While learning Dr. Gallo's technique and exchanging work with fellow students in class, my PTSD disappeared never to rear its head again. The process took about fifteen minutes. Next I eliminated my fear of heights in twelve minutes.

I was on to something significant here. And the best part? Since most sessions took less than one hour (often just minutes), I could actually do that procedure to make a difference for people suffering traumatic stress from many causes.

Now that I saw synchronicity in action in my daily life, when I was provided an opportunity to learn a new talk therapy style I interpreted it as a message from the Universe and I latched on.

That action made sense to me at the time even though I know that, in the case of treating long-standing issues, talk therapy keeps many people stuck.

Two things happen in talk therapy that prevent permanent issue resolution: (1) you can only access information using your conscious mind – and all the root causes lie deep in your subconscious mind; and (2) the more you talk about the problem the bigger it looms in your life.

Whatever you focus on expands. T. Harv Eker put it this way: "Where attention goes Energy flows."

Need an example? What happens if I tell you, "Don't think about a pink elephant"? Your subconscious mind does not process negatives so it hears and acts on, "Think about a pink elephant." The more you do think about a pink elephant the more you cannot stop thinking about the pink elephant – until something else distracts you.

As I contemplated beginning the new talk therapy course, I recalled a textbook included in my master's degree program.

Each chapter detailed a different technique used in psychotherapy. And each chapter ended with the words, "We used to believe that, but we don't believe that any more." I always wondered why the heck they bothered writing the book and, more to the point, why the heck reading it was a requirement!

Well, since I figured this new (to me) course was a gift from the Universe, I enrolled and made my way to Washington, D. C. every week to attend class.

Yes. I went into Washington, D.C. every week – with my eyes closed.

Do you wonder how I could walk through the streets of Washington, D.C. with my eyes closed? Do you wonder how I got to Washington, D.C. from my Virginia home?

I took a Metro train into the city. I counted the number of stops the train made so I knew when to open my eyes to get off the Metro. I didn't feel too safe in the area around the stop so I used my eyes to navigate away from there into the safe residential neighborhood where my class convened.

I could tell when I was walking by a building, a tree or a car. How? My hearing had become so acute I heard air moving. When I walked by different structures the sound of the airflow changed. I came to recognize different airflow patterns.

Cool, huh? Nature provides. When we allow ourselves to tune into the amazing Universe we then can take advantage of all the loving guidance coming our way in every moment.

By the way – my newly tuned-in hearing also awakened me to the non-stop sounds of nature and the rhythms of city life that always play in the background of our lives. Close your eyes the next time you go for a walk – in Nature or in the city, doesn't matter. You will hear a whole new world that only your subconscious mind knew about before.

Sweet harmony – when you pay attention. A cacophony of noise when you leave it to bombard your eardrums randomly.

The class I attended in Washington, D.C. wasn't as much a class as an internship where I practiced a new way of working with clients: in a room with a one-way mirror. In this environment, however, I found myself unable to implement some of my most powerful healing tools.

Virginia Satir, the founder of family therapy, told us that people need four a hugs a day to survive, eight to get by and twelve to thrive.

I believe the most powerful techniques for healing anyone of anything are hugging and touching; but those techniques are not allowed in many work places. Yes, I understand the legalities, and unfortunately I learned that sometimes it's not safe to be alone when working with clients who may become violent. But, when working with mentally stable clients, I was able to do my most powerful talk therapy privately one on one, implementing my nonconventional methods.

Another practice I use that makes sense to me (and not only for dealing with clients) is that I always thank the other person for sharing with me, and I tell them I really appreciated what I learned from them. I do this with everyone in my world.

I remember one young girl in her twenties telling me, "You learned something from me? Nobody ever learned anything from me."

Life is an infinitely expanding Learning Circle. Every person, with no exceptions – not even babies – has something to teach and something to learn. Pay attention and you will learn something from every person, pet, plant and the earth itself. Look for the wisdom or you will miss the treasures life throws your way daily.

To give you an idea of the power of the work I did (and do) instead of conventional talk therapy – the Energy Dx & Tx I learned from Dr. Gallo – I will share a story that I hope will open your eyes to your own possible healing, at least on an emotional level.

One of my clients at the Washington, D.C. facility came in to see me. She had always been a lively powerful presence. Today she presented as a meek unhappy quiet shadow of herself. When I asked what was going on this incredible story poured out.

She was homeless, as was her boy friend. They were engaged to be married. That part I knew. She then shared what happened since our last visit.

Recently, the boy friend learned the government owed him a huge sum of money – so much they were out shopping for a house and a car!

He was her best friend, the love of her life.

She quietly revealed he had taken ill suddenly and died a few days earlier. So not only did she lose her best friend, her love, but also a new lease on life.

Forty-five minutes later she smiled. She confided that she thought she could never smile again because that would not honor her lover. And now there she was back to herself – smiling and ready to be in life again.

In forty-five minutes she recovered from a major life tragedy because she was ready and wanted to change and I knew how to help her – not by talking about it, by doing something about it.

I get so high when I work with someone. I hear the smile in his or her voice if we are on the phone. I witness the smile in person. I LOVE what I do! No wonder the Universe continues to take care of me when I feel lost or scared. My work is very important for very many people.

My work? Every day I ask the Universe to use me to do It's healing on at least one person. I serve as a conduit. I think all "healers" do.

Rarely, but sometimes, I work on animals too. After all pets come to us for specific reasons. Treasure your animals and listen for the messages they deliver.

All of my life, from the age of five, I knowingly caused smiles to blossom. That is what I do. And that is why I know about happiness.

Coming to this paradigm of energy work certainly counts as one of the biggest gifts of the injury. Hey, I never knew this whole field existed prior to my need for it.

From Dr. Gallo I learned about meridians and acupressure for the first time. I discovered how each meridian (energy highways that traverse the body – long used in Chinese medicine) carries a specific emotional theme and each point along each meridian addresses an even more specific aspect of the emotional theme for that meridian.

It is no accident that Dr. Gallo's work fit niftily with what I was learning from Carolyn Myss and Reiki practitioners about chakras.

My healing network spread in ever widening directions. I learned modality after modality seeking to heal myself. Par for the course.

Did you ever notice that most, if not all, healers came to their work in an effort to heal themselves or a family member? I surely did exactly that too.

Observe how guidance from the Universe came to me so clearly.

Each class usually ran one week at a time – one week of long days packed with very intensive learning and hands-on experience every step of the way.

Remember that I had no short-term memory. Yet I was often the first one in my classes to comprehend the material. The fact that I could not hold on to the information did not matter, because every modality involved using open manuals!

My point? Clearly the Universe was showing me my new path. Not only did I grasp information and the how-to quickly, I also applied it with great success when I worked on people myself.

My lack of energy limited how many people I could treat. No matter. I found miraculous results with 100 percent of the people who came to me for help.

How I Know My Results

As I mentioned, I do before and after checks to evaluate the status of the entire body's organ systems, and I always make sure all systems are working before a person leaves my table. I am not saying all fifteen systems stay at 100 percent for long until we have cleared the blocks that interfere with deep and total healing of the physical and energy bodies.

For a while I called every healing a miracle until I realized that all I did was remove blocks to healing allowing the body to do as Nature designed it: heal itself. No miracles needed!

Do you know that energy blocks begin in the energy body and only come into the physical body when they do not get cleared out in the energy field?

Did you ever have a muscle knot that was terribly painful to the touch but the doctor or massage therapist said you had to push hard on the painful spot to relieve the problem?

Those spots are blocked energy that manifested as physical knots because no one knew to find and clear them when they still existed only as energy.

When I get to the second traumatic brain injury – following surgery to remove a brain tumor – I will go into detail about energy blocks impacting the physical body.

Chapter Eight

Powerful Thoughts

Remember how I stopped the suicidal thoughts?

Change happens instantly. The space between your ears carries more power in your life than the sum total of the knowledge of all the medical and alternative healers in the world. You invite wellness – whatever wellness means for you. OR you invite some other degree of health or the lack thereof.

When I work with someone who is ready to change the issues disappear immediately – usually in three to four sessions with me.

They make noticeable celebration-worthy changes after each session along the way.

AND I want to be very clear that when I work I feel very guided about what I do. I feel love, wisdom and healing channel through me. I serve as a clear and open vessel through which the Universe can work.

Normally I do not like being used. Yet every morning when I mediate I ask the Universe to please use me to do Its work here – to make a positive difference in at least one life today. I make that request every day.

You don't have to be in the healing field to do that task. I feel every person is here to help others in whatever way they can. And for some of us that help may be in smiling or saying hi when passing by someone walking down the street.

Realize that when you make a difference in one life, you impact every person in that individual's world. Either those around him or her change to fit in with the new way of being for the person OR others who do not want to change themselves at all drop out of the changing person's life.

For the most part, family and friends like the status quo. So when you change (especially true in the case of moms) the family often wants you to change back. Hey, they don't want their comfort disrupted.

Look at divorce statistics of women married more than thirty years. Ask them why, after so many years, they chose to end the marriage. You will find consistency in the responses: mostly around a lack of honor and respect – not recognizing that mom is a person with her own needs that get put on the back burner and rarely, if ever, get satisfied.

Why?

Because when mom takes time to self-fuel the family calls her selfish. Or because mom doesn't speak up to let her family know what she needs.

When anyone suffers a brain injury, the family cannot possibly understand the experience of the injured altered person. Especially in the case of closed head injuries – no one "gets" that Mom is struggling and needs NOT to take care of others but to be cared FOR by others. They need to be told.

The brain rehab center I attended offered a talk for family members of TBI survivors. My family did not attend. My children were away at college at the time, and when they did come home for visits, no one understood that my life had changed dramatically. I had not yet chosen to speak up for myself. I did not explain what had happened to me and what my reality had become.

I failed to make my own wellness important to them. I didn't know how.

Wake up. Taking care of yourself is about being your best, being your healthiest, and feeling terrific. Then, and only then – when you are fueled spiritually, physically and emotionally – can you give to others without life force draining resentment.

By the way, that fact holds for every person, especially all moms and women in general. You do not need to suffer a TBI to feel used, taken advantage of and invisible as a person.

My readers write to me asking how to stop being a doormat more than they ask any other question. The problem is not uncommon *and* it is society-based.

Quick side note: why do you think so many women get breast cancer and other female cancers? What function do the breasts serve? Nourishment. Of whom? And the uterus and ovaries? Giving birth – but to whose dreams?

If you wonder how that remark fits in know that every ailment, every injury, every condition, and every disease results from a very definite pattern you live out of your awareness.

When I do an evaluation for people I give them the entire picture of their patterns – physically, emotionally and spiritually— so they can stop, prevent and reverse the damage before it takes them out one way or another.[10]

What I want you to realize is that one symptom may be the result of twenty different causes. A doctor who fails to think outside the box or take sufficient time to talk to the patient and get a picture of his or her entire life, but instead quickly hands out a drug prescription to hide the symptoms, may not help you at all.

---

[10] Visit my webpage to understand how I work and why what I do makes a deep and immediate impact for people – who are ready to change.
http://www.howtobehappywithalib.com/how-i-work-1/

Thank goodness for the doctors who really care about their patients and reverse the damage done by others.

Chapter Nine

Deceptive Appearances

What I am about to share may seem very odd to you. Please stick with me because this information may well save you from a major life injury.

Very Hard To Believe
And Probably Very Illegal

I knew the facility where I worked was an unhealthy and an unsafe place to be – both because of the design of the building and because of some of the behavior I witnessed in my coworkers.

The supervisor in the crisis care facility scheduled mandatory "social" gatherings for all employees. At one such "party" in someone's home with spouses/partners present, some of my colleagues used real names of clients and called them crazy!

Geesh! That truly vexed me. For one thing, they violated the privacy of the clients. They also slandered them.

Despite what happened to me, I know a person's soul is whole and perfect. And even though a person seems to be operating in a strange realm where they inflict harm, on a soul level no one is crazy. Their human behaviors may be terribly out of whack; but crazy? Not in truth.

Remember you live your life through appearances rather than actual events. Your spin on events gives you the interpretation of good or bad. Others, witnessing identical events – evaluate events differently than you do.

You may find it hard to believe but I never felt anger toward that person who attacked me. My family and friends were so angry – but not me. My life turned upside down and inside out, yet in my eyes she gave me one of the greatest gifts of my life up until that time.

I knew I had to leave the facility and took no action. She conspired with me, on a soul level, to take me out of that life so I could discover who I am and why I came into this lifetime – which is precisely what happened.

If that scenario does not make sense to you please re-read that section. Understand that even horrific circumstances are gifts. They are actually requests your subconscious makes to the Universe; and the Universe ALWAYS responds to manifest your requests in ways that serve your highest and best interest.

I knew I needed to leave but I took no action to do so. So the Universe, which grants my every request (and yours too), answered my prayer and took me out.

The Universe didn't just take me out of that facility. It took me out of talk therapy completely. I had to make that transition so I could help more people more quickly, deeply, and permanently.

What You Don't Know About Affirmations

I addressed the topic of choosing which paradigms to believe in. I now want to address the topic of affirmations.

When done accurately, affirmations may serve to speed healing. Affirmations always work. The problem is most people have no idea what they ask for – all day long.

Generally, people tell you to speak your affirmation first thing every morning and last thing every night because those times tend to allow messages to enter the subconscious mind and by-pass the gate keeper, your conscious mind.

Two problems here:

1. The gurus tell you to speak in the present tense as if the event already happened. But in doing so, they unknowingly teach you to use the language of the conscious mind rather than that of the subconscious mind. The conscious mind understands statements that are stagnant and fixed, such as "I am healthy and happy." The subconscious mind hears and absorbs statements that are active, ever growing and changing, such as "With every breath I am breathing I am gaining more and more health."

In order to get a message into your subconscious mind, you must speak the language it understands.

2. Most people speak their affirmations and then live the opposite of what they say they want all day long. They negate the positive affirmation by outnumbering its recitation and attention with negative thoughts.

For example, within my own experience, if I speak, "I am easily and comfortably swallowing whatever I eat" but then each time I drink or eat something I worry about whether or not I will swallow it or wind up choking, then I send out the message about choking more often than I do the desire to swallow easily and comfortably.[11]

The reason you keep living what you don't want is that you focus on what you don't want all day long. "Where attention goes energy flows."

The Universe, not knowing good or bad, always gives you what you ask for. Always. If you do not like the way your world looks ask yourself, "What would I have to be thinking to attract this circumstance into my world and cause my life to look like this?"

---

[11] For complete details on how to speak affirmations consciously and in the language of the subconscious mind, I highly recommend my CD set, *Ali On Goals and Affirmations*. See the Resources page for details.

Then focus on what you *do* want instead of what you do not want. The only reason to look at your current disempowering thoughts is to know the opposite thoughts to generate and speak.

Remember, what you focus on expands in your life.

Chapter Ten

What I Discovered About Your Health

Remember I told you the injury altered many areas of my functioning? As I studied specialized kinesiology modalities, I found certain facts to be common among pretty much all people; but neither the medical community nor the general population has a clue about any of it.

Whether or not you survived a major trauma I know these facts about your health right now:

1. You are dehydrated
2. Your TMJ is out of alignment
3. Parasites feast on your innards
4. Heavy metals roam your body

I could write a book about those health issues. Right now I will describe how each of those conditions blocks healing.

The signs of dehydration go way beyond thirst to actual conditions (emotional and physical) and disease.

Fatigue happens when the body gets dehydrated. Instead of running for a caffeine fix when you feel tired, get a glass of water – water that your body will actually assimilate and use. As a hydration specialist I know that most people are two quarts short of the water their body needs to function at an optimal level.

You cannot live in radiant health without drinking enough good water daily.

Your brain is very vulnerable to stress from many different sources. Since it runs your body you want to know how to keep it healthy by eliminating stressors.

Your body is electromagnetic. What do you need to conduct the messages from one neuron to the next? You need salt and water. Your body is 75% water. Your brain is 85% water.

Your brain takes up about 1/50 of the whole mass of your body. And yet it uses 1/5 of the water you take in.

Now what does that tell you about water and mental functioning? Have you noticed how many people, surprisingly some of them are only in their twenties, joke about their senior moments, or their brain fog, or what they forget?

Chances are it is dehydration. Most people think about drinking when they are thirsty. By the time you notice the thirsty sensation, you may already be dangerously dehydrated.

How can you accurately pass a message from cell to cell if the water is not there, and if the salt is not in the water? Think about that one for a moment. It cannot happen.

You need to eat ¼ teaspoon of salt over the course of the day for each quart of water you drink so your body can actually use that water.

If you drink the right kind of water, at the right pH with the right amount of oxygen, you do yourself a big favor by promoting brain healing. You are also aiding prevention, as you will be less likely to get sick, get hurt, or develop emotional conditions as easily or as seriously as you will if you fail to consume enough water and salt.

You can dramatically improve many aspects of your health simply by changing your water- consumption habits.

Following the injury, a friend observed how terribly out of

breath I became simply by walking a flight of steps. My heart was pounding and I was puffing away and dizzy.

What conditions do those symptoms remind you of?

My friend called a heart specialist she knew and made an appointment for me to go see him and to get a stress test ASAP.

Dr. Batmanghelidj, a physician in Northern Virginia, has been practicing for over thirty years. His big cure is water.[12]

He went into a hospital where a man could not be helped by all kinds of medications and all kinds of procedures. Dr. Batmanghelidj gave the patient water and the patient got better almost instantly.

We are talking about a whole gamut of emotional things going on. Most emotional issues resolve, not with psychotropic drugs, but with water. Almost all pain, other than something from an actual injury, is due to dehydration.

You may remember back from high school biology how water gets in and out of cells? It does that with salt.

So this whole thing about salt not being good for you and causing high blood pressure – do your research. Discover the studies that led to the stop-easting-salt craze. Do your research for yourself.

As a practicing Specialized Kinesiologist I can show you why your body needs salt when your heart starts beating too fast, and you are panting and running out of breath going upstairs, and your legs get weak and your kneecap hurts.

You see, I had all those symptoms and went to a cardiologist (which I highly recommend you do to rule out any actual heart issues). But all my tests showed nothing abnormal with my heart or

---

[12] Dr. Batmanghelidj is the authority on water and hydration. At his website, http://www.watercure.com you will find the information you don't know that you don't know about water and dehydration.

with its functioning.

I was fortunate to discover a chiropractor who practiced kinesiology and demonstrated to me that all those symptoms resulted from a shortage of salt. As soon as he gave me salt all my symptoms disappeared and to this day, when those symptoms recur I test myself to see if I just need more salt and so far, more salt and more water has corrected those symptoms every time.

Headaches, migraines, all kinds of things are happening because you do not have enough water and salt.

Edema. What about when you have swelling going on? That is because the water cannot get into the cells. It's outside the cells. You have two oceans in your body: one is inside the cells and one is outside the cells. Do you know what? I could go on and on because I actually give a forty-five-minute talk all about water.[9]

What I want you to take away from this right now is the fact that when there is not enough water in the right places, the brain rations the water that is there. So what do you suppose happens? Gradually the brain shuts down the less vital functions. You may then develop discomforts, conditions and ultimately disease.

If you already suffered a brain injury, then your brain is inflamed. Toxins find a home in that inflammation, as do parasites. You need water to wash away all that mess.

As a specialized kinesiologist I know the importance of water. In fact, in my very first session with clients I clear the energy blocks most people have to assimilating and using water.

The common advice to drink eight glasses of water daily and go to the bathroom every 1½ - 2 hours makes sense if your body experiences water running right through it.

The fact is, when you drink enough water that your body actually uses you need less and will make fewer bathroom visits.

Most people tell me they drink lots of water. They emphatically insist they drink enough every day. Yet when I spend time with them I see how very little and how infrequently they drink plain water. More importantly, I see health issues arise in people that I recognize as dehydration – issues which doctors call illness, and for which they prescribe drugs.

No other liquid gets absorbed or utilized for a myriad of health issues the way water does. Your health, in fact your very life, depends on your cells taking in adequate water every day all day long.

Oh yes, you need water and minerals (salts) that allow your body to absorb the water. Without proper mineralization and without breaking down the sticky water molecule (water tends to clump in groups of sixty molecules), you cannot function at 100% or enjoy optimal radiant health.

How To Calculate Your Daily Water Requirement

Take your body weight. Divide that number by two. You need that many ounces daily. For example, a person weighing 100 pounds needs to drink 50 ounces (6+ glassfuls) over the course of the day.

The best way to make sure you drink what your body needs is to measure out the entire amount. Put it in a bottle. Then pour your servings from that bottle all day long. Once the bottle is empty you've had enough. (Unless you had alcohol or caffeine, experienced high stress or sweated a lot - then you need more.) For every cup of caffeine or alcohol you need two to three glasses of water to reverse its dehydrating effect.

Oh yes, if you drink soda know that carbonated drinks steal so much oxygen from your body that for every ten ounce can of soda you need thirty-two glassfuls of water to restore that lost life-giving oxygen.

Do you see why so many people experience brain fog and have trouble concentrating?

You are an electromagnetic being. Without adequate hydration the messages that run your system will fail to transfer accurately eventually perpetuating current issues while creating new serious health issues.

Beyond the physical exhaustion I experienced from the dizziness, my low immune system left me open to develop an autoimmune condition presenting as an excruciatingly painful scaly rash – psoriasis.

Nothing touched that rash for four years until a special water system, one that turns sink water into Pi Mag living energy water, came out. Within days, two days to be exact, the rash started clearing and was all gone in two weeks.

Signs of dehydration that people fail to recognize as dehydration include skin rashes.

What You Don't Know About Your Jaw Joint

My jaw joint, the Transmandibular Joint that you may know as TMJ, sustained the full brunt of each blow that night in June. What you likely do not know – most doctors and even dentists do not know this either – is that your TMJ is responsible for 80% of your neurology and 90% of your muscles.

That foot, ankle or hip pain, the memory, headaches, and learning disabilities, and a host of other symptoms simply reveal a misaligned TMJ. As a specialist in jaw alignment I see major life changes happen instantly when I energetically align the TMJ.

Consider the fact that sustaining a head injury inevitably involves knocking the jaw out of alignment. Heck, it is very easy to move your jaw out of place and not even know it. All you have to do is get your teeth cleaned. All those positions in which you hold your jaw while the hygienist cleans and protects your teeth pull your jaw muscles out of alignment.

Tooth health is imperative to whole body health. Make sure you keep your dental cleaning appointments. Just learn how to re-align your TMJ yourself.[13]

Many people do not feel clicking or pain when their TMJ is out of alignment. Their pain may be in many places other than at the TMJ!

For me, the short-term memory I lacked for three years came back instantly when a fifteen-minute procedure re-aligned my jaw. Why didn't my dentist who treated TMJ or the chiropractors I saw know a misaligned TMJ can impact memory?

Parasites Feasting On You

Everybody has parasites. Usually they are too small to see – but not always. Since most people do not have healthy guts (whether or not you know it your gut suffers many problems) parasites have a field day.

And they live all over your body not just in your intestines.

A simple fact I bet you didn't know that I trust will motivate you to do something about parasites: one third of what you eliminate daily is not even yours. One third of that gunk comes from the parasites that thrive inside you!

Super yuck!

Interestingly, parasites are low vibration organisms. When I work on someone, I cannot do my energy work at a high fast vibration to kill the bugs. I must move my energy level to their level. Matching their low frequencies allows me to wipe them out in minutes.

That is how a Rife machine works, too. It matches frequencies. A Rife machine, used to treat various diseases

---

[13] I teach classes on how to realign your TMJ. Please refer to the Resources page for more information.

including cancer, can be programmed to the exact frequency of the parasite or illness you want to eliminate. The machine then sends that frequency into your body.

Does it make sense to you that parasites, who find paradise inside your body, contribute to fatigue?

I have a theory that many people who suffer TBIs have a particular parasite in them. The symptoms, so common to all TBI survivors, match what candida does in the body. For me the worst symptoms were exhaustion and brain fog.

I had candida.

Candida is a very dangerous life-threatening parasite when it mutates into a fungal form and makes its way through the body. I find it all over the body when I work with people – and I do mean everywhere, including the brain.

That brain fog you experience just may be candida. It may be other things too. Know that candida is a major culprit in a wide range of health issues that baffle many doctors who usually cannot pinpoint the cause for diarrhea or constipation, flatulence or brain fog, vaginitis or fatigue.

The list of symptoms range from itching to sores, skin problems and a weakened immune system. Left undiagnosed or improperly treated (as is usually the case) this parasite gets labeled chronic fatigue syndrome, leaky gut (and the gamut of digestive upsets for which people visit the digestive-aids section of drug stores with great frequency), muscle and joint pain and stiffness, allergies of all kinds, reproductive and urinary tract conditions, vision issues, brain fog and memory problems, and a host of psychological issues including anxiety, sleep disorders and depression.

That diverse array of symptoms often sends sick people to many different specialists who do many different tests and often prescribe many different drugs when, in fact, that single parasite causes all those different problems.

Unfortunately, candida is only now coming into awareness in the medical community at large. Hey, better late than never, yes?

Candida belongs in your digestive tract in small amounts. It eats heavy metals. Candida does not feed on sugars and mushrooms (also called fungi). That is why candida diets do not work. They do *not* eliminate the fuel source that allows candida to proliferate.

Candida eats heavy metals. In people diagnosed with MS, candida is commonly seen concentrated along the spine where heavy metals often accumulate.

Make sense?

Thankfully, after four years of suffering and sticking diligently to an anti-candida diet (which was useless, except that I was really thin that whole time), I visited an energy practitioner and my candida was killed in minutes. Unfortunately, that practitioner forgot to also program my body for a gentle die off – something I do when I eliminate candida from a client.

Still, the twenty-five hours of flu-like fever and discomfort that followed were bearable – way more bearable than having candida, for sure – and the fatigue diminished too.

Normally yeast grows in your intestines. In the numbers that Nature intended, candida poses no threat. However, stress, either from the brain not working properly due to injury or illness OR from emotional indulgences, can cause that yeast to go wild and overgrow – not just in the intestines but throughout the entire body, including the brain.

Really important for you to know, when a doctor prescribes an antibiotic you likely know how critically important is to also take probiotics as antibiotics wipe out the good flora along with the bad bugs. You probably do not know that candida attacks the liver and pancreas within 72 hours.

When a candida (yeast) mass reproduces itself, it releases formaldehyde in the body. Some of that gas reaches the brain producing the effect known as brain fog. Confusion, vision issues and memory issues result from that unwelcome gas.

How do you get rid of that discomfort and avoid the many dangerous health issues it can lead to? First of all know that it feeds on heavy metals.

If you live on the planet you have heavy metals in your body. No matter how strictly you follow the popular anti-candida diets out there you will not eliminate your yeast overgrowth with that diet.

You must get rid of the heavy metals that feed it. And you must do it safely so they do not spread throughout your body.

A specialized kinesiologist can prepare your elimination organs (which includes strengthening the involved muscles) before going after the candida.

Never kill candida without preparing your elimination organs first. Second, the practitioner should know how to command the body to make the die-off easy and comfortable rather than put you through the flu-like symptoms that I endured.

Your healthcare specialist can direct all the heavy metals out of their hiding places all over your body and then direct them out of your body. After clearing out the heavy metals and preparing your organs then you can eliminate the candida safely.

Then you get to pay attention to your handling of stress so you can prevent a re-occurrence of that uncomfortable environmental condition.

Candida, with the potential of interfering with normal brain function, can rob you of your health and happiness.

How do you suppose I became an authority on the subject?

I share what I know so others will not suffer the debilitation and discomfort I did for four years. Not a single doctor had a clue what was going on or what to do to help me other than prescribing statin drugs. For many doctors, vaginitis is a yeast infection they treat with statin drugs.

Candida is NOT a statin deficiency. Drugs will not remove the cause. A specialized kinesiologist ended that misery for me and gave me back a normal life. I can now do that for others.

When I eliminate candida and heavy metals in clients I feel like I am releasing the happy energetic person who had been trapped inside my client. Talk about causing smiles to blossom – theirs and mine.

Candida takes a very heavy toll on one's overall health. Other parasites do too.

I do this routine myself and I recommend it to family and friends as well as to clients: at least twice a year, do a colon. I have been eating well for forty plus years. I don't eat junk. I rarely eat processed food. I usually avoid sweeteners – including honey and maple syrup.

Given my healthy eating habits over the past forty plus years, the amount of gunk, including mucoidal plaque, that I eliminate during this very special kind of cleanse never ceases to amaze me.

Most of the cleanses out there, in fact anything that disrupts your daily routine, is not doing a proper cleansing and likely is not eliminating mucoidal plaque.

To encourage you to follow through with the colon cleanse (for starters and then the whole body cleanse) consider that your gut is holding an average of eight pounds of fecal matter that has probably been accumulating there all your life. Imagine the amount of toxins and parasites inside that mess!

When I do my cleanse I lose that little protruding stomach – that people call a pooch. My flat stomach returns. Pounds of gunk leave me, carrying massive toxins and parasites with it.

Remember, I've been eating healthy for forty plus years. Yet I still had the buildup of garbage.

That build up of fecal matter contains parasites that are feasting on you. Remember that one third of what you eliminate is actually garbage excreted by the parasites inside you. YUCK!

If knowing that fact doesn't get you to immediately order a healthful colon cleanse that doesn't upset your daily routine, you may as well stop reading this book. You cannot enjoy clear thinking and optimal health while hosting parasites and accumulated toxins.[14]

Sleep Matters

Old age does not make people infirm. The fact that their body has been shutting down since about the age of two does! And it all happens in such tiny increments no one notices the decline.

Sleep matters. People do not get enough of the restful, restorative sleep they need to maintain wellness.

In an injured brain, sleep deprivation slows down the brain's healing process; and in a seemingly normal brain, it leads to less than optimal brain functioning.

The only time your body gets to repair damaged cells and replace old ones with new ones is during sleep – deep sleep. Most people believe they can function on only a few hours of sleep each night…

Wrong!

Somewhere around the age of two the brain notices that it expends so much energy every day it needs more restful repair/grow-new-cells-time each night than it gets.

---

[14] Go to http://BlessedHers.com to educate yourself and find out how to purchase the only colon cleanse I use and recommend. Get the Colon Cleanse Kit not the kit not the 5 Day Revive cleanse

The brain runs the show, yes? It takes what it needs.

Just as the developing baby takes what it needs from the pregnant mother for its growth, regardless of how their taking impacts mom, the brain takes what it needs as top priority – regardless of the impact on the body.

So, the subtle deterioration that begins some time in year two of life reflects the gradual and incremental shutting down of organs in order to feed the brain.

Studies reveal that people need between seven and ten hours of sleep for health each night, depending on which reports you read. The average American gets less than six.

Thirsty, malnourished and sleep-deprived brains cannot function in top form. In fact, they cannot function for long. Period.

Magnets: Essential To Health

Your body is electro-magnetic. Without water *and salt* neurons cannot accurately communicate with each other. Salt-water conducts electricity but plain water does not.

The second part of that equation – the magnetic piece – explains why, as earth's magnetic poles shift and the amount of magnetic energy available to humans declines, many diseases (known as magnetic deficiency diseases) appear in the population.

I don't know about you but if I do not pay attention when someone says something, I may simply take it in and believe it and apply it in my life.

That is one reason my healing took three years, at least I see it that way.

Soon after the injury I found online support groups for people who survived TBIs and were in the healing state, as well as sites for caretakers of people with TBIs.

As I mentioned, on one such site I learned about magnets and their ability to aid in healing the brain.

I love the way the Universe works. My masseur knew someone with magnets – but not just any magnets. The person did a technique using magnets on my body while I rested on a magnetic sleep system. That technique simulated sleeping on that magnetic sleep system.

I investigated the company and the product and wasted no time getting one into my home and on my bed. I did sleep well on it but I didn't see a big change in my brain for a while.

I feel somewhat embarrassed to share the reason why I failed to get a quick response.

I attended a meeting where people shared more information and personal stories about how they used these special magnets to heal all kinds of health problems and injuries. And someone described the sleep system as feeling like lying on the street with your head on the curb. She remarked about how hard that contoured pillow with the magnets felt.

I believed her and suddenly the pillow felt too hard for me to sleep on. Odd, don't you think, that I had not felt that way before that night?

I stopped using the pillow. Since that time the company redesigned and crafted a soft comfortable pillow and mattress topper that most people prefer – comfort wise.

What I did not know is that the top part of my mattress on which I slept those three years (where the magnetic pillow would have been) had no magnets in it!

There I was looking for magnetic impact for my brain and not giving my brain any magnetic exposure – at night, anyway!

ARGH!

Three years later I attended another meeting where a woman stood up and said, "The pillow really isn't that hard. I sleep fine on it and by the way, there are no magnets in the top part of the mattress where the pillow goes."

That night I pulled my pillow out of the closet, put it on my bed and slept well.

Two weeks later the severe fatigue vanished completely.

I vividly recall the day I felt better, the day I knew the fatigue was gone forever. If you suffer from fatigue from a TBI pay close attention and know you can heal. You *can* get back your energy. I did it and I know how to show you how to do it too.

You know how you sometimes have good days, days when you feel better and want to squeeze in as much activity as possible because you have no idea if or when you will get another day when you feel this good?

And remember every time you fill that day with activity you deeply regret it the next day?

I am with you!

I lived that way for three years. And then one day I packed a week's worth of activity into my feel good day. That night I hit myself in the forehead with a, "What the heck did I do? Now it will take me one to two weeks to recover!'"

Only I awakened the next day still feeling good. And, well admit it, when you feel good you forget what it was like to feel bad, so you go on and live a normal day – like you used to – and you do it without thinking, right?

The same thing happened that night when I realized I had done it again. Oh man! I was so sure the Universe would make the next day a big time payback.

On the next day I still felt good. On day three I realized I was better. I realized I had healed the major cause of the severe fatigue.

Magnets relax muscles – tight muscles holding the TMJ (and therefore the skull bones) out of alignment. The magnets relaxed my muscles allowing my skull bones to return to their natural position.

In addition, the magnetic sleep system (which includes a high tech comforter) induces a profoundly deep sleep. The body only heals when in that deep sleep state. The more deep sleep I got, the more healing I did.

Happily, when I added a far infrared-magnetic sleep mask to my sleep routine my hormonal balance improved. Plus, I was able to sleep better even though our bedroom never got totally black.

Ah! It just hit me. The brain only releases melatonin when the room is black dark. Melatonin balances hormones. No wonder the black opaque sleep mask impacted my hormonal balance positively.

I love the way the Universe works – even when it does so without our realizing exactly how or why.

I met a man online who used magnets to reverse a condition that kept him in a wheelchair and caused seizures. He told me how to place the magnets in a headband and to wear them over my temples and at the base of my skull.

So I duplicated what was working for him. Wowsers! It worked for me. In fact, it worked so well for me when I talked on the phone or did teleseminars, my friends would speak up letting me know when I wasn't wearing my headband because there was a noticeable difference in my communication!

Yes, I know that we only need to know what to ask. Then the Universes shows us how to make it happen through synchronistic events and nudges toward specific actions.

Doing everything I just shared with you helped me eliminate the very many contributors to the severe exhaustion. After three years of dragging around, I was now home free.

Well at least I thought I was well on my way to recovery – finally daily living was not such an all-encompassing effort.

And then my mom's brain got hurt.

I am not certain what happened. My mom had become depressed with schizophrenic symptoms five years earlier – at least that is what the doctors said since, in their paradigm an eighty year old does not get schizophrenia. That happens only to people in their late teens or early twenties.

In the vernacular of today's youth, "Whatever."

What I knew was my mom lost her ability to care for herself. She was like a two-year-old child and I didn't realize that until I took her into my home to care for her.

Watching your mom deteriorate mentally is painful. Watching her waste away and not understand why created unfathomable stress for me.

Here I was, having gotten free after three years of intense daily struggle just to make it through each day. Now this was supposed to be my time to focus on myself and on what I wanted next in life.

I chose to be a stay-at-home mom at a very young age, and I had spent the last 21 years of my life raising my two active kids. Being a stay-at-home-mom was the most important and rewarding choice I made. I learned so much raising my children and really enjoyed the time I spent with them. But now that they were away from home and in college, I was ready to live my new life for the first time!

Only I couldn't do that.

I was having a real pity party for myself. Then the Universe delivered this message to me, "It is never about you. It is always about the other person."

In that moment I stopped thinking about myself. I thought about how my mom was suffering. I spent the rest of my mom's life holding her hand and being with her – three months of pure love.

During that time there were moments when my mom looked me in the eye and spoke as my familiar mom rather than my unaware confused mom. One especially difficult day when my mom wouldn't do what I needed her to do (get in the car and out of the rain) she said to me, "You're the only one who takes care of me."

You see, no matter how things appear to be, the Spirit is always present and perfect.

My mom, despite being like a two year old, knew how I treated her, how I took care of her, and most importantly, how much I loved her.

Taking care of my mom during her last ten months was the toughest job of my life. It was also the most wonderful gift for me. I got be with her – without anything interfering – totally with her.

Oh but it took its toll.

When she finally transitioned out of her pained body I was able to let go. I was able to acknowledge how much effort and strain I had endured those last ten months of full time care.

The emotional pain equaled the physical output for me.

When she left I basically collapsed.

While I did not feel the same kind of fatigue I had previously conquered, I was pretty much exhausted and unable to function well for months. Frankly, I am not sure if that was because my brain was still healing or because the stress would have left anyone in that state.

Interestingly, the day after my mom left this world, the county from which I was medically retired called to say they had a job for me and if I did not go do their office job they would stop the disability retirement pay that had made up for my no longer being able to work.

I told them I would not and could not do the job they wanted me to do. They said I would have to go to the state capital and go through a court case and win to keep my retirement status.

Let me tell you about the jobs they put me in prior to this ill-timed command from the powers that be in that county, acting with zero comprehension or wisdom or heart.

First thing they did was put me in the other crisis care facility – like my emotional state could deal with that kind of stress.

This facility was way more unsafe that the first.

Get this, the staff office was on the interior with no exit in case of emergency. Wait, it gets even better. The staff used yellow tape on the doorjamb of the split door. They kept the bottom of the door closed. And a sign warned clients not to cross the yellow line!

Are you kidding? Did they think someone in a psychotic episode would stop and read a sign and say, "Oh. I can't go in there. I will leave now."

The thought that any door could stop someone in such a rage is a joke – except the consequences would be anything but funny.

When I saw the unsafe environment I really freaked and told the nurse who was working with me that she had to get me out of there. The supervisor in that place also told me I had to come in on the day when the rest of the staff would be in court – leaving me alone.

I told my nurse that was not going to happen. And she told the county that was an inappropriate placement for me.

Next, the county put me in the county records center working on a computer all day. The doctor helping me with my vision specifically said I could not work at a computer and here they were disregarding the doctor's orders.

Guess what? The Universe works perfectly – only I sure do hope I didn't screw up any innocent victims.

I was supposed to sit at a computer all day and input court case numbers, locating the files in this massive record keeping facility that served this huge county of one million people.

At that point, I had no idea I had developed dyslexia. No one checked my work. I have no idea if what I typed was accurate. If I made any mistakes, those records would never be found.

The Universe always knows. As my heath status declined severely and quickly sitting at the computer, I asked the doctor to remind the county of his orders and I was out of there. It took me a while to recover lost ground from the experience.

Okay, so next they put me in the county building in some department where I was to answer phones and direct the calls to the appropriate employee. The phone system was so complex I didn't stand a chance of connecting any calls – let alone calls that came in concurrently! Besides, the county building was enormous, fancy and busy. The stimulation completely overwhelmed me!

Their attempts to get me working hugely set back my healing. I guess that is par for the course for a government program.

Taking yet another position the county deemed right for me was not even a remote possibility for me. I had to let go of the notion of challenging them rather than appear in a court at the state capital.

What a grossly unfair action they had taken. In fact, all the actions they took were unfair and counter-productive. Clearly that county system was a very unhealthy place to work. I was ever so glad to leave it and move away when I got the chance.

A lawyer I spoke with said I absolutely deserved my retirement. But a friend who had gone through a similar event told me the damage to her physical health was no way worth the possibility of winning.

Between my emotional and physical state I chose to let it all go – and to trust the Universe to lead me where I needed to go to serve my purpose here.

Wow! So first I suffered the devastation of having to give up my dream to be a psychologist and now I was definitely out of the work place.

Of course I came to see that was the best news of all!

There is a difference between being happy and living a comfortable life. Choose to be happy now.

Chapter Eleven

Everything Happens Perfectly Despite Appearances

All good. Again that lesson blared in my mind, "Everything happens perfectly. Look for the gift."

Admittedly, with all the exhaustion and emotional upset of the past ten months – losing my mom slowly and steadily – I just didn't see any way except giving in and trusting the Universe to lead the way.

When you fail to heed the messages delivered in whispers or act on the gentle nudges the Universe yells at you. I just didn't want to get pummeled again – not ever again.

Forced to quietly retreat within and lay low to recoup my energy, I spent more time understanding how the body, mind and spirit work together. I had to understand how to heal myself. And I had to know how I could help others both prevent and reverse whatever obstacles kept them stuck.

I spent the next fourteen years learning everything I could about the mind-body-spirit connection – about the how and the why. I learned many different modalities figuring out what worked and what didn't work as well.

I put together the pieces and formulated my own way of working, my own modality. And I began working with clients using my own style.

One day, three years ago, as I was clearing someone suffering with severe and widespread candida, I notice my fingers began to go numb on my left hand.

As the days went on the numbness crept up my hand, my arm and eventually up around my neck and down my right arm into my hand.

Soon the only way I could hold anything was to look at my hand and my fingers and the object and tell my brain what to do while I made my hand do what I was telling my brain to do. Muscle memory at work!

That worked fine while picking up objects; but when I only had two fingers feeling the steering wheel - that scared me. That is when I started seeing alternative healthcare practitioners.

People just do not expect a person to have a brain tumor. Even when I saw someone who specializes in the brain she did not check for a tumor.

Finally a chiropractor and an acupuncture doctor suggested I get an MRI to eliminate the possibility of a tumor and see what was happening.

I recall the last client with whom I worked. I recall those sessions well because I was working with mostly numb hands and though she didn't say anything, I am pretty sure I poked her in the eye while I was working.

When the numbness showed up briefly in one foot I knew it was time to do what I had feared and got an MRI.

There I was trying to find the place to vote when my cellphone rang and the acupuncture doctor (who had convinced me to get the MRI) told me the imaging showed a brain tumor that extended down to my top cervical vertebrae. Good thing it did because I had gotten a cervical MRI not a brain MRI.

He told me go right back to the imaging center for a brain MRI.

Without going into detail, I saw the MRI showing a sizeable tumor wrapped around my brain stem and the top two vertebrae in my neck.

Included in that tumor were three major nerves and the right carotid artery. I knew about the artery. I did not know about the nerves.

What did that mean for me?

The neurosurgeon warned me that I could awaken from the surgery unable to talk or swallow. He didn't tell me about the other possibilities. Take my word for it, those two bits of information sufficiently sacred me.

I wrote my will and called my kids and brother. Only my daughter got here in time to be with me before the surgery. The others couldn't get there until the next day.

The neurosurgeon described a surgery that routinely took eight to ten hours. He said, because of the size and location of the tumor, this surgery might become a two-day operation and he explained exactly why that possibility loomed overhead – literally.

I got my house all clean and in order so I could tell anyone where to find anything I might want should I wind up staying in the hospital a long time.

I asked everyone I knew and who knew me to send Light and Love, to say prayers and to visualize the tumor sliding out as if my brain stem and vertebrae were non-stick Teflon.

I assume that is precisely what happened since the surgery only took four hours.

I continue to feel grateful for every person whose lives I touched and who definitely touched mine too. I know I say it often but: I LOVE the way the Universe works.

Well, I woke up after the four-hour ordeal unable to talk or swallow. I choked on whatever mucus was happening and on my own saliva. Since only half my mouth worked I had to use artificial saliva on the non-functioning side and then choked on that too.

I also could not move. The pain was surreal. Even the morphine pump didn't touch it. I couldn't move and worst of all – everything was still numb regarding my hands and arms! ARGH!

Honestly, I wished I had not survived. I could not begin to imagine how I could live when I could not breathe because I could not swallow. My own fluids were smothering me.

I didn't know there were three important nerves inside that tumor. When I heard I might not speak or swallow I had no clue that was just the beginning of what else would not work.

The pain from the damaged nerves that ran across my face and through my eye just added to the misery.

I really could not understand why this happened. And I need to know why things happen.

I went from the hospital right into the rehab center inside the hospital so I didn't need transportation that took me outside. I honestly felt like my head was going to fall off every time I moved. To this day, when I lie down or sit up I hold my head and move it with my hands as my neck muscles are still not back to full strength.

You know how these days the nurses get you up and out of bed as fast as possible? When the nurses came to move me into a chair I discovered all the muscles on my right side had instantly atrophied. Seriously, I dropped ten pounds – of muscle weight.

It turns out some of the nerves that were cut and partially removed controlled many muscles on my right side. Without orders from my brain the muscles could not function.

I am right handed. Do you see a problem with not being able to do things efficiently with the right side of my body?

The neurosurgeon told me no amount of physical therapy could restore the lost muscle function since the nerves enervating those muscles no longer worked.

Another paradigm I chose not to buy into.

I had not just lost my ability to talk or swallow, I lost my ability to walk. I did learn to walk, talk, and swallow – even if not the way I used to.

There I was a young sixty year-old pre-surgery. People usually guessed my age anywhere between forty-five and fifty as I had been very fit and (I thought) super healthy. Suddenly I found myself in the body of an old sixty year old.

I wanted to scream and cry only I couldn't. My eye hurt too much. I didn't want to it to tear.

Thankfully, immediately after awakening from surgery my daughter slipped the symbols into my socks that Krystalya Marie had channeled to help me release the toxins from all the medications used in the procedure and those that would later invade my system in the aftermath via the morphine pump that theoretically handled my pain. Frankly, the morphine didn't help much. I know I never want to know that kind of suffering ever again!

What a huge gift my friend gave me with those symbols. Since I use written words placed on the body in my own work, I know well that the body sees and acts on anything and everything touching it. Without those symbols the toxicity would have been greatly multiplied slowing my recovery.

Okay. So I got through the days of feeling very down. I was so scared but I also figured if I made it through the surgery, and if the eight to ten hour surgery only took four hours then the Universe had plans for me to not just heal but to do lots of good in the world.

I am going to digress a moment here. This is, in my opinion, very important for you to know and to look across your life for similar messages.

I just told you I knew the Universe had plans for me, big plans: to allow me to do the work I came here to do.

Just take a look…that night, June 9, 1996, that attack could definitely have taken me out. And then there was the blizzard.

I was driving from Virginia to Georgia for a class. It was March so I didn't expect snow and chose to take the route over the mountains rather than the eastern route down I 95.

I was hurrying to leave home before it got dark so I didn't take time to remove the snow shovel from the car.

I wore sandals – open sandals. After all, I was heading to Georgia in March.

As I drove into the mountains it started to snow. I was lost and stopped to call a friend for directions. Thankfully he answered the phone and told me where I needed to go. I later learned he was worried about me when he didn't hear from me again – with good reason – I had driven into a veritable blizzard – no exaggeration.

The snow flew fast and heavy. I was moving along at twenty miles per hour while crazy drivers whizzed by me! I do not understand why people think themselves immortal and drive carelessly and fast on snowy roads. Even the big trucks went barreling along past me.

As I drove, I saw cars off the road, down ditches – all along the way. Then it happened. It was my scariest moment behind the wheel.

I hit an icy patch and my car spun out of control. I feared winding up down the embankment where other cars had gone. And then, I know this was because the Universe was taking care of me, my car stopped just off the road and facing in the right direction at the top of a steep embankment.

Another miracles happened in those few moments. During the time I was spinning out of control not one single car or truck came down the road. Had one come along that would have been the end of me.

That snow shovel that sat in my trunk came in handy.

I got out of my car. Still no one came along so even though I was shaking life a leaf, so shaken from the experience, I cleared off my car.

As I finished clearing off the car and a path back to the road along came a car and a young man asked if I needed help. I told him I was fine.

Ready for this? I had been out in a few inches deep of snow shoveling – wearing open sandals and no head cover in a blizzard. When I got in the car I was absolutely dry - my head, my coat, and my feet – all dry.

And when I had to get back on the road no traffic came at all. As soon as I got safely back on the road and back to my creeping, probably less than 20 mph now as the blizzard had worsened, I knew the Universe watched over me. I knew, again, I was here to make a difference for those three million I had set as a goal years before.

So now I had three signs from the Universe that I was never alone plus I am here to serve my purpose and am totally supported in doing so.

You see, as hard as every moment has been since the brain surgery, I always know I am okay. Sometimes I may not feel too okay. I spend a lot of time telling myself, "This too shall pass." And I know everything happens perfectly.

I learned that lesson while caring for my mom during her last ten months as an undiagnosed cancer ravaged her body and stole away her mind. I go into detail why I know we are always whole and prefect in my books about mental illness.[15]

I knew to look for the gifts and, being who I am, I also needed to understand why I had two brain traumas. What the heck was I doing? What lesson did I fail to learn and not seen the first time?

---

[15] You can find links to my books on mental illness in the Resources section at the end of this book.

Chapter Twelve

The Second TBI

My studies revealed that tumors happen when someone fails to forgive someone or something.

Forgiveness is a big deal with me. I actually created a ritual in my ministry to physically forgive and release the emotions caught up within.

When you do not forgive someone for an action you interpret as hurtful you cause a small energy block.

Earlier I explained how blocks begin in the energy field and only enter the physical body if they are not handled in the energy body.

So I understood why a tumor. Even though I had done the ritual for myself. I usually receive how-to info during meditation and then apply it to my own life before sharing it. This ritual was no exception.

I was so sure I had forgiven everyone in my life for every action I interpreted as hurtful to me.

Well, I assumed I had forgiven everyone and sent each of them love for moving me out of my comfort zone into a better life. Oh man, so many gifts – the most impactful, in fact – come very well disguised in packages so painful that they absolutely make you stop (often literally) and take notice.

The brain injury from the attack got my attention. The brain tumor now led me to see how very many people I had not forgiven, had not thanked and sent love their way for whom I got to become because of what they did in my life.

For me forgive means for giving love to those who came into your life to make you so uncomfortable you get to grow and change to remedy what they did that hurt you.

I made a longer list than I had previously, recalling every incident ALL across my life where I interpreted an event as hurtful.

My list stretched seven pages long – and I write small. And even then I missed someone really significant. I had not forgiven myself for so many incidences where I thought I hurt someone else.

Before going any further, let me explain what I believe about forgiving.

Events just are. They have no meaning in and of themselves. People assign a meaning and interpret events as being good or bad or neutral.

If you look across your life, or better yet, ask those close to you if you ever did anything that felt hurtful to them, you will likely feel great surprise at what they share.

Firstly, most often, when you do things that someone finds hurtful, you have no clue they feel that way. You are not a mind reader and cannot know what hurts them if they do not tell you!

Secondly, if someone else does something that hurts you (physically or emotionally), you will want to check to see if you trained them to treat you that way.

When you allow behaviors toward you that you do not like, you send a message that it is okay to treat you that way.

In effect, you train people how to treat you certain ways. You also teach them to treat you by modeling how you treat yourself.

Let me give you a concrete example.

Do you have a friend who calls you to say she is passing through town and wants to come by to see you? You have not seen each other in five years and she will be here in fifteen minutes. You go into the kitchen and take out two teacups and an assortment of teas. And you are ready for the visit.

You have a different friend, same last minute call for a visit as she passes through your town. Only this time you rush about straightening the house, hiding stuff to make the place look neat and presentable.

How come the different reactions to the unexpected visits?

The first friend taught you she likes to kick back and be with you and doesn't care a bit how your place looks or whether things are in their proper place.

While the second friend has let you know she likes a home to be neat and clean and expects order of some sort when she comes to visit.

So if someone in your life is not treating you the way you need right now – and recovering from a TBI dictates certain needs you probably never had before (especially help with doing things you used to do without thinking twice) – then you need to speak up and ask for what you want and need.

Also, tell people what you do not need, for instance, loud music or music that seems loud now that you have sensitive hearing.

Get the idea?

You are in charge of your healing.

No one wants to hurt you. If you experience behaviors that you interpret as hurtful tell the person while the person does that thing. They do not know their behavior bothers you. They probably do not want to hurt you at all. They probably feel really bad their actions caused you any upset.

Just know they cannot know such things unless you tell them.

Also know that no one can damage you – not the real you. You are a Divine Spirit. No one can possibly do anything to you that can come even close to touching your Divinity. No one can damage who you are or how your Spirit is.

In addition, anything they did that you interpret (the key word being *interpret*) as hurtful happened because you allowed that action into your life.

Before you get all excited and start reacting, listen to what I mean.

People come to Earth to experience some kind of spiritual soul growth by going through life lessons. More often than not those lessons come through painful experiences.

When a huge lesson needs to happen two souls agree, before ever incarnating, on coming into this lifetime together. They love each other so much that one soul agrees to be a horribly awful person who does something really bad, maybe even horrific, to the other person giving the perceived victim the chance to take the action that leads to learning the desired lesson.

Now, is the perpetrator doing something good the victim requested and agreed to? They became the teacher – even if by inflicting pain.

When you look at people who survived awful experiences (emotionally or physically) you will find them thankful for the experience that changed their lives – the experience that flipped the switch to turn on their great life.

If you take time to look at every single person and incident you think hurt you all across your life, and if you really make the effort (it is easier than you think once you start the process), you will find something for which to thank that person. You will find who you had to become and the unfamiliar action you had to take because of how they treated you.

They gifted you so you could grow and become who you are now.

You see, the true meaning of forgiving is *for giving love*. When you can see the gift and thank that person you then send love to them.

No, you do not have to go to that abuser and say, "Thank you." You do this process for you. If doing it on your own just is not cutting it for you then contact me.

Trust me, you do not want a tumor to grow in you!

I realize this whole notion sounds crazy. When you actually do this exercise you will feel its power.

If you fail to forgive, you hold the hurt inside and it literally poisons your system. You release damaging chemicals that destroy your health and happiness. You create energy blocks that can grow into tumors.

Please understand my message here. If someone exerts physical abuse they physically hurt you. In the same moment they give you a chance to make the choice to leave.

Having worked with abused women I *know* that choice is difficult and scary as heck. I understand the mind and brainwashing that an abuser creates, and the fear that even the thought of leaving that deadly situation may cause.

Still, that person forces you to make a choice that you might not otherwise make – the choice to stand up for yourself not in confrontation, in leaving the situation – with help.

Okay, so I understood the tumor. But why in the brain? And why was my brain my center for serious life altering change?

A tumor grows where your major issue lies. Every point on your body (and energy body) involves very specific emotional themes. The brain serves as mission control for your life. Specifically, I was not living my truth. I was not doing the work I felt in my heart I came here to do.

I spent my life taking care of everybody else's needs instead of defining, clearly, my reason for coming into this lifetime.

Oh my gosh! No wonder the Universe yelled at me – twice. After the first life altering TBI, I still failed to chart a course to fulfill my life mission.

I also noticed that losing my voice magnified the fact that always speaking up and caring for and meeting everybody else's needs did not honor my own needs.

I gave up asking for what I needed and wanted because whatever I asked for never happened.

I often wondered if I was invisible and my voice too soft.

I recall a friend once telling me that I was like a lion when I spoke up in the book group to which we belonged. It was just that I didn't say much too often.

She told me, "When you speak everyone goes silent to hear what you have to say."

Hmm.

Interesting, don't you think? I lost my voice with the second brain incident. What a metaphor!

The completely amazing fact I found, living in not knowing whether or not any sound will come out when I open my mouth to speak, I speak anyway. My voice does not sound like it used to. Sometimes my voice leaves in the middle of a word.

I speak anyway.

Speaking and teaching live classes gives me a high I cannot begin to describe. People not only listen, they also participate in my experiential presentations!

For the guts to make videos and speak whenever I can locally, I give a huge thanks to Heather Picken. She told me how important my being as I am and doing what I do in this present state is for many people out there – to inspire them to go out into the world just as they are. Before Heather, I remained silent thinking no one would want to listen to me because my voice didn't sound so pretty.

I want you to know whatever challenges you face, the Universe put you in that position so you can grow through it. Not just grow through it but thrive.

I hesitate to label myself a TBI survivor. I don't want to just survive. Heck, if that was all that mattered I would have followed the lawyer's advice and filed for disability!

I made a conscious choice not to take that step. Why?

When I went to the government site and looked at the process for filing for disability I saw the words, the disability must be permanent.

I know too much about how the brain and mind work to proclaim my current health status as permanent.

Even if my body never recovers I refuse to send such a message to my powerful subconscious mind. I will not allow it to set up a file folder saying I am disabled – because then it will have to put me into situations that fulfill on that description. Your subconscious mind runs you – not your conscious mind.

No way was I about to allow a file folder to be created and filled with situations to validate my being disabled.

Do you grasp my point?

Over the years I talked with potential business partners who said, "No. I cannot make money because I will lose my disability." If that is you or someone you know then that is your choice.

It just is not my choice. I choose to heal. And healing, again, means accepting myself as I am now – not expecting to return to my former body and mind living.

Your life simply reflects the activity happening in the six inches between your ears.

Chapter Thirteen

I Discovered True Happiness

The gift I received from this newly (well, is two years ago newly?) altered body and brain surprised me – and I think at least a few others too.

One day, about six months after the surgery – still unable to swallow anything without severely choking, barely able to walk and struggling to get out vocal sounds – I found myself feeling high.

High as in how I feel when I workout and get the endorphins flowing! I was almost giggly high!

Looking at my life from the outside – heck looking at my life from the inside – it made no sense to feel incredibly great. It made no sense that I loved the world and everything and everyone in it!

Hmm. Actually it made a lot of sense. You see, I was living in happiness. This major trauma carried me into the realm of living in True Happiness.

What then, is true happiness?

Happiness has nothing to do with events. It is not about 'when he does that' or 'when I accomplish this goal' or even 'when I heal and everything works'.

None of that is happiness. All those things are events you interpret as making you feel good and you likely define that good feeling as happiness.

I know when I survey my readers and ask them what happiness is for them I get those answers: sleeping late on the weekend, a day off from work, going on vacation, etc.

I repeat: all those happenings are events that you interpret as happy. They have nothing at all to do with True Happiness.

True happiness is a lifestyle. It is how you live every moment of every day regardless of what happens in your world, unrelated to the situations or circumstances of the day.

Let me explain that concept in concrete terms – well, kind of concrete terms.

Assume that happiness exists along a scale of one to ten, where one means zero happiness and total dissatisfaction with life in all aspects; and ten is a life where you feel happy and successful in all areas of life all the time, even when seeming failures and dreadful events happen.

Everyone experiences bad things in their lives – everyone, no exceptions.

People get sick, they get hurt, loved ones move away, people lose jobs, relationships end, people die, and on and on.

No one escapes the traumatic events of life.

Let's take a person who lives a very ho hum life, not really excited about anything and unhappy and dissatisfied in some areas of life. They live life at a level three of happiness.

Their best friend gets a new job some place else and moves away. For the person left behind who lives at a level three of happiness, losing the everyday presence of that best friend feels like a six event (on a one to ten scale of bad things happening in life, where one is nothing bad ever happens and ten is the death of someone dear to you).

So, that person living on level three has a level six upset.

How do you suppose the level three person will deal with that level six upset? Probably not too well. Probably the level three person will feel great sadness, distress, loneliness and possibly even depression. His or her level of happiness cannot handle a level six upset.

Now let's say a person who lives at a level nine happiness experiences the identical situation – level six distress.

The level nine person will deal with the situation, feel the upset and still be okay – no life changes, no emotional devastation. They will feel sad – even deeply sad – and they will bounce back and take the level six event as a life event that happened.

Time to move on – not to forget the friend but to refuse to allow the event to ruin his or her life.

I have determined that I live my life at a level eight – and have lived here for a year and a half now.[16] Therefore, even when the surgeon told me the nerves will not regenerate, even when the doctors told me there is nothing that can be done to heal the dangerous situation in my digestive system, even when the speech therapist tells me my voice and swallowing may not return to where they used to be, and even when the rehab physical therapist tells me she doesn't know how else to help me move my right arm or run, jump or skip or hop… even with that huge disappointment (I have been very athletic all my life and those limitations come as a level eight blow to me), I know I can go on with my life.

I can still feel happy. I can still smile. I can still get high for seemingly no reason at all.

I realized I found the true meaning of happiness and taken up residence there.

One way I make it through the days when my functioning is not optimal is I set an intention to feel good. When I know someone is counting on me to give a talk or teach a lesson I intend not just to have a voice but also to be able to project my voice so everyone in the room can hear me and understand me.

To date, my voice has been there every time I needed it.

---

[16] Happiness levels can be determined with the use of self testing and tools such as pendulums.

I also learned that loving myself means not pushing beyond my limits.

I thank my coach, Joan Endicott, for telling me it is okay to leave an event *before* I feel bad, to be aware of my limits and honor them.

Whoa! What a difference that choice makes for me. My letting a presenter know I might leave early – or even being okay with doing so if I didn't get a chance to let the presenter know – to honor myself by leaving before I feel ready to collapse I no longer need to suffer fatigue or dizziness.

I thought I understood loving myself before. Now I really understand what loving myself is – what it means and how to do it. I will share how to do exactly that and why you must do it to heal from any situation in your life – most especially to heal traumatic injuries, be they physical or emotional or spiritual.

Something you need to know about healing and why you have issues that need healing…

Every physical, emotional, mental or spiritual challenge that happens in your world reflects disconnects. Those disconnects happen in three realms: (1) Between you and your True self or Spirit; (2) Between yourself and other people; (3) Between you and a higher power—no matter whether you call that power God, Source, Life Force, etc).

When I assess someone, regardless of the complaint they bring to me, I get information about which of those disconnects are at play in their lives.

One way I love myself is to give someone a card when I meet them – not a business card but a card that tells them where my functioning may be while we are together because I never really know how I will feel in a situation, especially when I forget to set an intention before the meeting and when I am in a noisy busy environment which is usually the case when I leave home.

On that card I let them know three things about me, as someone recovering from brain surgery:

- **If we are talking** my voice may or may not come out when I open my mouth and my diction may not be perfect.
- **If we are eating or drinking** together I have to focus on everything that goes in my mouth whether it is liquid or solid –to avoid choking. If I do choke, unless I raise my hand or turn blue, I will be fine in a moment
- **If we are walking**, when I come to a step or curb I have to calculate how to handle the up or down. If I have to walk a flight of steps please do not talk to me as I calculate how to handle each step.

People seem to appreciate knowing where I am. I am grateful I no longer have to try hard to keep up with them regardless of our activity.

You may have an invisible injury that forces you to muster all your strength and focus just to appear normal when you are out and about. I think letting someone know your state is helpful to you and to them.

Many people judge others (by the way, anyone who judges another speaks volumes about how they feel about themselves; think about that a moment and you will see what I mean), so you want to give your best first impression. Who would do otherwise?

Since my own brain damage changed how I speak, swallow, and walk, I easily recognize those limitations in others. When I wind up on the phone with a customer service representative who speaks slowly and not so clearly I am extra patient instead of feeling annoyed and asking for a supervisor. I think to myself what a courageous individual to take on such a demanding job!

The same holds true when I find myself behind someone who takes each step slowly and deliberately.

OH OH OH ! Please Pay Attention To These Words

Soon after I got out of rehab I had to send a very important letter by certified mail.

I was not walking well yet, not even with the walker but I had to do this myself.

My friend drove me to the post office. Much to my dismay there was no handicapped entrance. I could not open the door. All my muscles had disappeared and besides I could not let go of the walker to use a hand to open the very heavy door.

I stood outside as people went in and out. No one, not a single person, offered to hold the door for me! I had to step back to keep from being knocked over by people who seemed to be in a hurry to go no where in particular.

Thankfully my friend noticed my predicament. She came over and held the door for me. The same thing happened inside going into the mailing area. Same situation: no one holding a door.

And once in line, no one offered to let me go ahead of them.

As I stood in line not sure I would be able to speak, having expended so much energy waiting to get inside – I found myself fighting back tears. I recall telling myself, "This is what it is like to be handicapped."

I don't know about you, in my mind common courtesy tells me to hold doors for people and most especially to hold open a door for someone so obviously experiencing a mobility challenge.

I let people go ahead of me at the supermarket if they have a few items when I have many. It just makes sense!

By the way, the exact same thing happened at the grocery store despite the fact that the automatic doors stayed open. People rushed by me never giving me the space to enter (and later exit) the store.

I was grateful for the furniture department in the store that allowed me to sit down and rest for a time so I could make it back to the car.

Sounds silly but ask a friend to check if the store where you shop has a place to sit in case you need to. I got stuck in a store with no open seats. They had roped off every chair in the entire store. I nearly collapsed while there. I will never go back there.

I thought about all the people who live their lives this way every day – and I felt such profound honor and respect for every one of them. I want the world to know how amazing they are. After all they could simply choose to stay home and not venture out, not make an effort to improve their lives.

You know what? Every time I feel down because of what I cannot do yet, the Universe shows me someone whose life is more of a struggle than mine. I mean it happens instantly so I don't get to feel sorry for myself. Hey, self-pity never served anyone!

For years I thought my path went off in undesirable directions. I called them detours. Finally I discovered there were never detours. My path meandered so I could experience everything necessary to live my life as I do.

Chapter Fourteen

My Inspiration

Meet my inspiration who, just because I know her and her story, gets me through my toughest times. I met Bonnie Jensen a few years back when she was named Mother of the Year. When I read about her I contacted the local paper where I had seen the article and got in touch with her.

At the time I was writing parenting books and wanted to meet her with that thought in mind. But when I actually met her and her family – let's just say my life changed.

I met Bonnie before I ever knew about the brain tumor. And sadly she was out of town during the toughest part of my recovery. But, knowing her got me through and continues to get me through many moments.

I will not allow myself to waste energy or lower my frequency by feeling sad or angry for more than a few moments so I do not dwell in feeling anything that does not feel good. Feeling bad does nothing to further my life and certainly doesn't feel good.

What you focus on expands!

One of the amazing things about my friend is that Bonnie has two prosthetic legs. A rare disease led to that state. The remarkable attribute (well actually an endless list of remarkable attributes make Bonnie so special) is you wouldn't know there is anything different about her. She is the mother of five adult married children with twenty-two grandchildren – most of whom live locally, as does her aging mom.

Not only does Bonnie help out her family regularly she also is very active in her church. Though we do not share the same religious faith, I love to hear Bonnie speak. She is brilliant and easy to listen to because she always speaks and shares from her heart.

Bonnie's husband, Norm, is also a very special person in my life. With deep gratitude I call them my dear friends. They are so there for me, helping me with things I cannot easily do for myself.

In particular, when I feel limited or frustrated all I have to do is think about Bonnie and how she makes it through life without complaining (well, at least as far I know – Norm may know something else).

If I call or email Bonnie, as busy as she is, she responds to me. Just knowing she is in my life makes a difference I need when my mind and body get stressed from over-doing.

You don't need to suffer a traumatic injury to overdo and feel overwhelmed and exhausted. I know that for a fact, having been a "stay-at-home" mom of two active children.

Another special couple comes to mind when I notice feelings of not being happy arise. Ann and Gerry Hendrix hold a special place in my heart. Partly because following the surgery they came to see me frequently when I was at my worst. Heck, I even had a feeding tube up my nose back then!

Synchronicity brought them to the hospital to see Gerry's mom. Kindly they spent time with me too and occupied my mind making my misery subside all the faster. They too help me out with all kinds of needs I cannot take care of myself – yet. Perhaps the most important is the blocks Gerry made to raise the head of my bed. Paralysis in my digestive tract causes a severe acid reflux issue that prevents my sleeping flat. His effort plus Ann's help placing the blocks makes for a life-saving gift.

When feelings of not being happy arise, I picture Ann's warm smile. Ann has physical conditions that cause her much discomfort yet, like my Bubby, Ann usually has a warm loving smile on her face. She never complains about anything. She just does what she needs and *wants* to do.

You Have to Be a Good Friend To Have Good

Some of the greatest blessings of my life come in the form of friendships. Before the first TBI I ran myself ragged being super woman – caring for my kids, volunteering everywhere, taking care of my home and my mom who lived nearby.

I know the supermom syndrome affects many women still today. I also understand the hormonal imbalance that drives women into that state. But that is story for another book.[17]

When the attack left me unable to get myself to doctor appointments or just be unable to leave home, I had to learn to allow others to do things for me. That was so hard to do!!!! If you are a super woman you know exactly what I mean.

That is a very unhealthy way to live. I never could have healed from the first or second TBI had I not given in to allowing others to take care of me.

A wise woman once said, "every woman needs a wife." I agree.

Learn to love yourself first and maybe, by honoring your being and taking care of and *knowing* your hidden programs, you may never have to feel the power of the Universe's two by four.

The Universe always speaks first in whispers and then gentle nudges before ever getting loud. When you fail to acknowledge

---

[17] See resources at the end of this book and get a hold of Dr. John Gray's book, *The Mars and Venus Diet and Exercise Solution: Create the Brain Chemistry of Health, Happiness, and Lasting Romance.*

them (likely because you do not know how to listen or see them), the Universe has to get louder and more and more in your face.

Carolyn Myss says when lots of things go wrong in your life it is your angels knocking you off the couch! That is a pretty good description of how I felt – twice.

I recommend learning to hear the whispers. And I definitely recommend loving yourself first to avoid any need for further disconnects.

I think, at least, that when you resolve the disconnect between you and your True Self, then those between you and other people will likely fall away as well.

The disconnect between you and a Higher Power will also resolve. You see, Love is the solution to every problem. And it all begins with your love for you.

Chapter Fifteen

Loving Yourself First

I spoke about living in happiness and knowing True Happiness. Now I want you to know the first step in reaching that place where stress will not take you out of the game – except temporarily at most.

Loving yourself first – not just loving yourself but putting your needs ahead of serving the needs of everybody else – is a prerequisite to happiness.

I am pretty sure that's part of the reason I didn't call for help during the attack. I had no clue that loving myself was an okay thing to do. I didn't want anybody else hurt so I let myself be the target.

No, I didn't stand there with that fist knocking me repeatedly thinking what I just said. Your subconscious mind runs you. It was those programs that stopped me from calling for help.

I thought I had to do it all myself!

You must love yourself first. It is not selfish. It is mandatory.

Happiness Happens When You Love Yourself First

You came to this lifetime to live in abundance – not to suffer. Yes, you can learn lessons without suffering. You learn them faster with some struggle.

I can tell you first hand, having been through more than one life-threatening event, you can definitely learn without the serious pain. I finally reached that place.

Why does happiness matter?

People, like everything else, are energy – Divine Beings (pure energy) living human experiences in physical bodies. You are not your bodies or your minds. You are Spirits, Souls – eternal bundles of energy.

Energy vibrates at different frequencies. Higher frequencies move quickly in tall waves. Everything good and happy exists at those higher frequencies. Everything that is not good – the things and people you seek to avoid (like parasites) – all vibrate at low frequencies.

When you love yourself first, you live in happiness. By law, you attract *who* you are and *how* you are in life. You attract things and people whose frequencies vibrate in harmony with yours.

Love vibrates at the highest frequency. God is *love*. When you love yourself first you attract all that vibrates at high frequencies. Your love impacts others, the community, and the planet.

You cannot give what you do not have. It is not possible to love others – not if you really stop and examine love – unless you love yourself first.

Does what I said so far make sense to you?

The more love you give away, the more love comes back to you. But not just love. Everything that is good comes back to you when you give love. Again, you cannot give love unless you love you.

Until you love you, you only know *about* love. You must experience love to know it. You must *live* love to know it.

When you do love yourself, you cannot withhold your love. It exudes from your every pore. You wouldn't want to stop that from happening. You could not stop it, because it feels so good to you.

Loving yourself first is not selfish. It is mandatory. Selfish is not doing what you want to do. Selfish is expecting others to do what you want them to do.

Happiness naturally happens when you love you first. Giving to others becomes something you enjoy because it feeds good too.

Whether you are healing from a traumatic injury or not, nothing in your life will work, nothing will flow smoothly without bumps, until you absolutely put you first in your life. Without self love you lack self-respect and self-honoring. What you do not feel for yourself you cannot give to others – including honor or respect.

The thing is, you cannot fulfill your desire to live in happiness until you create love for yourself. You gotta love yourself first.

Okay, so what happens when you love yourself first?

You create new programs within your subconscious mind. Your frequency increases to the level where everything you desire exists: the feel good emotions, friends, jobs, things, etc.

Everything is energy - everything, including you and me. All things are also energy. Thoughts are energy. All energy vibrates at specific frequencies.

Feel good energy vibrates at higher amplitude waves (think sound waves from your high school physics class) that move fast. When you feel good you feel energetic and happy. Sad and negative emotions and experiences vibrate at lower amplitude waves and long slow motion.

No matter how many techniques you use to create instant happiness you will never stay in that energy without making the internal shift to love. When you live love, everyone in your world will act differently toward you. In fact, your love will flow out, surround and fill others.

Yes, your love will flow into and surround others raising their frequencies to new heights too. Yes, the way to change relationships is to take care of you.

The only thing that keeps you stuck in the muck of daily living is your lack of self-love. The same holds true for those with whom you feel disconnected or even angry.

The person who you think you are merely reflects your self-image. Your self-image reveals the programs others installed in your subconscious mind when you were too young to filter out messages that did not serve you. Those programs, operating out of your awareness, run your life in every moment.

Self love means knowing your True Self – who you were at birth. When you know your true identity, as opposed to the person you define yourself to be, you cannot feel anything but love. You live in constant gratitude for every little thing in your world. You automatically see how the Universe supplies all you ask for at precisely the moment it serves your highest and best interest to accept it and allow it in to create your new reality.

Make sense?

You either love someone or something, or you don't. There are no shades of gray. Just as you cannot be a little bit pregnant, you cannot love a little bit. Love carries no conditions. Regardless of what someone says or doesn't say, does or doesn't do – when you love that someone you love the person and see him or her as separate from his or her behaviors.

Where are you on your love yourself first barometer? Do you know your True Self? Do you participate in the daily communications your True Self shares with you? Do you even know how to hear or talk to your True Self?

When you love yourself first you will only allow others to treat you with honor and respect at all times. Knowing, very clearly, which behaviors you will accept and which do not fit into your life style allows you to choose only relationships that fulfill your desires.

I am talking about both personal and professional behaviors. Remember that how you do anything is how you do everything.

Feeding your need to love yourself causes you to feel endless love for everyone and everything in the world. Love pours from your every pore with no conscious effort on your part.

You become one with love – and one with God, Creator, the Universe, whatever term you prefer. After all, God is pure love energy.

Remember that you teach others how to treat you by example. You model acceptable behaviors toward you. When you take time to eat well, get rest and enjoy recreation, you show others they must feed you well, let you get your sleep and allow you to just plain have fun – as opposed to taking care of them all the time while ignoring you and your own needs.

Know anyone like that?

You will only live in happiness when your self-love raises your vibrational frequency so high that you attract only and all people and circumstances that feel good.

Feeling good clues you in to the fact that you live in the present moment. All of your energy, taken to support you in the present moment, empowers you to stay healthy, which in turn supports optimal functioning of the Life Force that is you.

Life only happens right now...and now...and now. If you recall past memories you steal energy from your present moment, energy that your physical and emotional bodies need to get you through the day. The same holds true if you find yourself "living" in the future.

You need your energy *now*. You want to stay focused on *now*.

If your body and/or emotions come up short on energy right *now*, they go into your organs to pull what they need. Then, if you fail to get adequate sleep to replace all that borrowed energy, your health slowly, without your awareness, begins to deteriorate.

Loving yourself means knowing the past is gone forever. Loving yourself means the future is not here yet and just needs planning (not dwelling) there.

Loving yourself is all about doing what feels good for you.

No one likes to be around people who are self-centered, self-absorbed or selfish – no one. That kind of person does not have friends. They fail to put out the kind of energy that attracts feel good people and situations.

When Krystalya Marie interviewed me on A2Zen.fm, we explored how the mind-body-spirit connection shows up in peoples' lives AND how my work clears the resulting suffering. I shared the fact that I had recently discovered the true meaning of Loving Yourself.

My words came in response to a caller who sounded terribly down on herself. She said she must not love herself because she couldn't attract good happy things, only feel bad things into her life. And the intensity of her struggle continued to escalate.

Until you love yourself enough the Universe cannot make you privy to the mess hidden out of your awareness that causes your suffering. You will not be able to handle the information without self-love, self respect and self honoring.

In other words, when you have so much love for yourself that you can make it through heavy duty momentary pain, then you can free yourself forever.

What the heck am I talking about?

The Universe never presents you with a situation without also presenting possible solutions. AND you also need to be in a place where you will allow those solutions into your awareness.

I noticed this exact pattern working with clients for fifteen years. Some people's issues came with great details revealed by their spirits during our work. I never asked them to recall memories because the whole point is the deepest pain lodges out of your awareness where it remains inaccessible to the conscious mind.

I also noticed that some clients' spirits gushed forth with minute detail all across their lifetime. Yet other clients only flitted through those moments so I could catch them and enter them into the circuits I worked on; yet we never knew the details of what happened when.

In both cases, the clients cleared the suffering for the specific issue on which we worked each circuit. Yet those who got to know the causes were the ones ready to handle *and dismiss* the emotional attachment to those issues.

The others knew the ideas and emotions of the root causes but did not experience the same opportunity to know what they cleared. That outcome left them vulnerable to repeating the patterns. Working together we disclosed the emotional pattern just not *how* the pattern showed up for them in real life instances.

When you love yourself, the Universe throws stuff at you because It knows you are ready to heal as soon as you "get" the message that the Universe has a major life lesson for you. When you fail to hear the message delivered in whispers it gets louder and louder and more in your face until you find yourself in crisis.

Major ouch!

Faith and trust: without those loving concepts in place nothing moves you forward into the unknown.

Chapter Sixteen

Happiness or No Happiness: Choose

At some point in time (not sure when) mankind – at least in Western society – switched the dominant default mood from our birth right of happiness to one of struggle and negativity.

Witness the look on most people's faces as you pass by them or simply remain still and observe what you see everywhere. You will see more anger, wrinkled brows, or sadness than you will smiling bright faces. Mostly, though, you will notice ho hum looks that seem to say, "Let's just make it through this day."

Consider these statistics: you think 65,000 thoughts each day. Of that 65,000, 95% are the same thoughts you thought the day before – and the day before that and the day before that ad infinitum.

Now add to the mix the fact that 80% of those daily thoughts represent negative events or imagined negative situations.

You don't have to be a mathematician to understand how that huge thought form enveloping far too many people on the planet is one of scarcity – not being enough or not having enough of this and that and everything.

Also realize that only about 2% of people actually think.

The remaining 98% ask their friends and family for advice when they need to make decisions. They do not bother to seek expert advice for things like where to bank, what kind of insurance to get and through whom, where to live and shop, which doctors to see, etc.

Very important life decisions, then, get made eac day by people who choose not to invest the energy or effort to take responsibility for their important life decisions. How do they benefit from their laziness? They have someone to blame when things fail to work out as they hoped they would.

Hmm.

With so many people not thinking, the majority of the energy from which to draw comes from negative viewpoints of life – all of which elude man's nature, namely, love. People who live on automatic buy into the huge thought forms of lack.

It is impossible to experience two opposing emotions in any single moment. So anyone thinking of what they want that others already have (envy) will not simultaneously feel gratitude for what they *do* have. Neither will they experience joy and love for the other person who has what they themselves want.

What if you decided to live in gratitude?

What if you saw love every place you looked – because actually, every place you look love does exist. You choose whether or not to allow that love into your life.

You expend more energy to feel good than you do to feel bad.

What?

The default energy you experience vibrates at a low and s-l-o-w frequency. You can only attract experiences and things that exist in frequencies in harmony with your current level of vibration. Therefore you must raise your energy level higher to get what you say you want.

Notice I said, "what you say you want. " The bottom line truth is that you have what you want in life in every moment. Affirmations totally work. The problem is most people have no clue how or what they ask for.

Want to know what you ask for every day of our life? Look at your life. What you see reflects your requests.

Which brings me back to my initial point: of the 65,000 thoughts you think every day, a full 80% are negative.

How can you change that state and plug into the life you desire? Live consciously monitoring your thoughts. Catch yourself when you feel bad. Your feelings reveal your thoughts that operate out of your awareness.

Make sense?

What one step will you take today to make the difference that will shift you into happiness so you can live the life you desire? You can do it instantly. It doesn't have to take weeks or months.

Just do something different NOW.

You Are As Healthy As You Think Yourself To Be

Whatever you think about your health and level of happiness determines how healthy and happy you actually feel.

In his famous book, *As A Man Thinketh*, James Allen quoted the Bible when he stated, "As a man thinketh in his heart so shall he be." Henry Ford reiterated that point in simpler language saying, "If you think you can or if you think you can't you're right."

What pictures do you hold of yourself in terms of health and happiness? You may or may not know, actually. You see, when you were too young to filter out their messages, your early caretakers (your parents, siblings, teachers, friends and society) created the picture you hold inside you out of your awareness, telling you who you can and cannot be, what you can and cannot do, and what you can and cannot have.

Consequently, the limiting picture you live by now, your self-image, only allows you to accomplish actions that fit that narrow definition of you. The good news is nothing about your self-image is set in stone.

You can change many aspects of who and what you are simply

by deciding who and how you *want* to be in life. You just need to know that fact, really believe it in your heart, and live from that truth. Decide, and then act in the new way – the way a person who lives the life you desire to live, acts.

How do you do that? Ask yourself, "What would a person who leads that kind of life have to do to be that way and have what they have?" Then work backwards. Ask yourself, "What kind of actions would he have to take to get where he is now?" Next ask, "What would such a person have to think that leads him to take those particular actions?" Finally, ask, "What kind of person takes those actions?"

Okay, so now you have some answers to some of those questions. Now what?

You could make yourself crazy trying to figure out all the how to make it happen, OR you could ask the Universe, God, Source, Creator (whatever term you use) to show you how to become like that person who already lives that other life style to which you'd like to become accustomed.

OR you can find someone who already lives that way and ask him or her to mentor you.

Actually you don't really need mentoring, per say; you really just want to follow that person around for a few days, note what they say and do, then do as they do while *becoming* a new you.

When you duplicate the actions of a successful person and you know in your heart of hearts that you deserve that same success, then you have to achieve that goal. Period.

Note that simply replicating their actions will never get you there. You must start in your heart and belief system. You must want and know you deserve that end. And you must take their actions as models and create you in your own way. You are not and never will be that other person.

You want to become similar to them, to take the actions that will get you your desired end.

Go for it. Be relentless and persistent. Take consistent action and move, always and all ways, in the direction of your dreams. You deserve to be happy

You may have noticed when I talk about my work I refer to pretty much instant healing. Well of course, because that is not just my paradigm but my own experience healing from the first TBI and working with my clients.

So the fact that the paralysis from severed nerves persists baffles me. Especially because there are times when I can swallow and speak. But truthfully, even when I look and feel better I still consciously do the work my body used to do automatically.

I know the first TBI caused nerve damage. Heck, I lost my short term memory for three years and could not reliably use my eyes or access my vocabulary. Hmm. Perhaps all of those challenges simply reflected the TMJ issue. I know that to be a real possibility. I wonder.

When I do not understand a situation I ask for guidance. I ask the Universe, my angels, and my guides what steps to take to change the situation.

I take steps all the time to move my life forward regardless of whether or not the paralysis resolves itself.

I have long said I write to see what I am thinking. So I finally answered my own question, now didn't I?

Healing is moving forward with my life as I am now. Period.

Whatever you decide to do with your life, or however you help a loved one living with a traumatic injury or aftermath, know how crucial this step is to the successful healing of any situation.

The sure path to health and happiness includes making a commitment to yourself to stick with the new routine until you succeed. Your good intentions will carry no power without that agreement.

Even if you make a commitment, that action alone does not

assure you will keep your commitment to yourself. In fact, right now your Commentator (that little voice that lives in your left brain ego mind) is telling your subconscious mind, "Here we go again. Yeah, right." And the files in your subconscious mind reinforce your past failed agreements you made with yourself.

What will be different this time?

Ask yourself how often you keep the agreements you make to other people? Do most people count on you to keep your word to accomplish something that benefits them? I bet you answered in the affirmative. So why don't you honor yourself that way?

Until you change that pattern and know that you alone can support any effort you make on your own behalf, find an accountability partner. Most people would rather do what they say than admit defeat to another person. The partner you choose will hugely impact your results.

Unfortunately, most friends or family members do not hold enough influence over how you feel about yourself to keep you on track. After all, they will love you anyway, whether or not you achieve your stated goal, right?

In addition, the possibility also exists that they may not be there to honor your agreed upon connecting time. Something else may come up for them and they figure you'll understand.

Has that ever happened to you or have you ever done that to someone else?

The fact is when you make that commitment to yourself with a big enough *why*, nothing – absolutely nothing on the planet – will stop you from achieving optimal health and happiness, as you define it for yourself. Until you reach that point, get a dependable accountability partner.

I recommend finding a coach. Study after study shows that when people invest in themselves they follow through. In fact, the higher the investment, the more quickly they succeed and the higher success they achieve.

When you don't put yourself out there you cheat those who need and want what you know and have and are already looking for what you do better than anybody else. There is only one you with your unique style.

Chapter Seventeen

How To Make Your Best Decisions

I offered you lots of information in these pages. I recommend you treat this book as a reference guide to help you sort through your own life. Apply what feels right.

Ah, but do not guess. Learn how to communicate directly with your Spirit – the immortal part of you that knows everything about you – past, present and future. You will always get accurate answers when you ask your Spirit for help.

How To Talk Directly With Your Spirit To Make Your Best Choices

To get accurate information with which to live your life without guessing, discover how to communicate directly with your Spirit. How and why do you access your Spirit?

Your Spirit is the part of you that connects to the All-Is-One.

Being the immortal part of you, it knows everything about your past, present and future. Sure, on an energy level, time does not exist and everything happens simultaneously. But let's focus here and now on the human plane.

Being privy to your soul path, your Spirit knows what actions serve your highest and best interest in every moment. For that reason your Spirit constantly guides you with messages you likely miss.

I teach you how to both receive and ask directly for what you need without using tools. After all, messages come at you non-stop, guiding you to live your happy healthy life in every moment – not just when you make big decisions. You don't always have the time or need to pull out tools.

For example, what happens if you get lost?

You ask which way to turn. Ah, but you need to know how to "hear" the response. When I say lost, I mean on the roadway to a destination in every sense you choose to interpret "lost".

Unfortunately, most people have no clue that two-way communication exists. Nor do they have any idea how to access the incoming information. So they go through life guessing which choice will best serve their needs.

Some quick methods to access your main messages involve simple divination tools.

No, divination tools are not woo-woo. They reveal your Spirit's wisdom.

Those I have seen or used in the past include a pendulum, tarot and angel cards, rune stones and rune cards. You ask a question or hold the question in your heart then choose cards, toss the stones, or observe the movement of the pendulum.

Frankly, I grab a book (in the library or off one of my many book shelves) and open it to a seemingly random page. Always, the solution I seek gets revealed in the words I read.

What actually happens is your Spirit guides you to choose exactly the book or cards that carry the message you need in the situation. Or the tossing of stones reveals the information. Or the pendulum moves in the "yes" or "no" direction providing your answer.

Ever notice how perfectly the reading fits for you? Now you know why.

With the pendulum you ask questions that require yes/no

responses and see which direction it moves. Obviously you need to know your "yes" direction swing and your "no" direction swing to benefit from the movement.

And, most importantly, you need to know how to test and prepare your body so you get accurate information. If your energy is misaligned (which happens for many reasons) then the information you get may actually be the opposite of the intended message.

The same holds true before using books, cards or stones. Always make certain your energy is flowing as it is meant to *before* using any tool.

Guess what happens if your head is in a negative place before using any deviation tool. The response will be negative.

Quantum physics proves that the observer always influences the outcome.

So much for the scientific method. You see, simple mood shifts on your part will create vastly different responses. Framing the situation also influences the outcome.

What do I mean by framing? If your head is in a place where you see yourself as smart and powerful before taking an exam, you will achieve very different results than you would if your mind told you how stupid and incompetent you are when it comes to test taking.

Happiness is your birthright. The Universe gifted you with access to your True Self.[18]

Your Spirit is your True Self.

Imagine how different your world would look if you viewed it through the eyes of your True Self.

---

[18] For more information about finding your True Self and communicating with your Spirit -- and to find out how to work with me, please see the Resources page.

You always see what you expect to see and what you accept to see.

Afterword

Amazing isn't it? Instead of being my personal day of infamy, June 9, 1996 became the day I changed my life into a masterpiece I could share with others.

Truly, I shutter to think how my life would look now had I continued to plod along in my comfort zone.

Now you understand.

Your past does not dictate who you are. Rather, it contributes to HOW you are in life AND has nothing to do with who you are now becoming.

Resources

For in-depth information about water
http://www.healthyyouuniversity.com/water

Complete nutrition you are not getting from your diet: real food synergistic blends, NOT supplements.
Details at http://healthyyouuniversity.com/vit-min

You CAN align your own TMJ. I show you how.
http://healthyyouuniversity.com/jat-online

To get a total overview of the patterns determining your state of physical and emotional health contact me. The programs that run you lie deep in your subconscious mind. If you could simply think your way free wouldn't you already have done so? Struggle is optional. Contact me.
http://thrivedontjustsurvive.com/contact

For more information on how a high tech magnetic sleep system and the only magnets that actually support and not hinder your body may help you or someone you know contact me at:
http://thrivedontjustsurvive.com/contact

Discover how to protect yourself and your family. Register to watch the cyber crime protection webinar at:
http://addmeinnow.com

Ali On Goals and Affirmations CD:
http://www.howtobehappywithalib.com/affCD.html

How To Contact My Personal Healthcare Practitioners and Colleagues:

Krystalya Marie, http://www.empoweredspirit.com/

Dr. Todd Watts, D.C., Functional Medicine, Total Body Wellness, Meridian, ID, (208) 914-0710

Judith Allen, RN, The Heart & Relaxation Coach, Judith.MySynergy.net

Dr. Scott Gibbons, D.C., Bridgetower Chiropractic, Meridian, ID, http://bridgetowerchiropractic.com, (208) 846-8898

Dr. Yvonne Fedewa, D.C., www.elifeboise.com

Debra Temple, Idaho Institute of Healing, intuitive healer and teacher, http://iioh.webs.com

Theresa Schmitt, Meridian, ID, massage therapist, http://www.enhancelife.massagetherapy.com

Dr. Rose Thomas, N.D., specializing in thermography, energy practitioner, http://www.drrosethomas.com

Paula Heath, executive director Missions for Visions, missionsforvisions@gmail.com

Frank White, http://www.fawhiteandassociates.com

Bibliography

Batmanghelidj, Fereydoon, MD, Water: Rx for a Healthy Pain-Free Life (Audio Course) 1997 Global Health Solutions, Falls Church, VA

Batmanghelidj, Fereydoon, MD, Water Cures: Drugs Kill, Global Health Solutions, Falls Church, VA, 2003

Batmanghelidj, Fereydoon, MD, Your Body's Many Cries For Water: You Are Not Sick, You Are Thirsty! Don't Treat Thirst with Medications! Second edition, eleventh printing, 1998, Global Health Solutions, Falls Church, VA

Davis, William, MD, Wheat Belly, Rodale Inc., New York, NY, 2011
Davis, William, MD, Wheat Belly Cookbook, Rodale Inc., New York, NY, 2013

Gray, John, PhD., The Mars and Venus Diet and Exercise Solution: Create the Brain Chemistry of Health, Happiness, and Lasting Romance, St. Martin's Press, 2003

Perlmutter, David, M.D., Grain Brain, with Kristin Loberg, Little, Brown and Company, New York, Boston, London, 2013

Whang, Sang1990, Reverse Aging: Not Science Fiction, But a Scientific Fact, Sang Whang, Miami Florida

A Gift For My Readers

People call me The Queen of Overcoming. Having read my story I imagine you understand how that reputation came about. I thought you might find it helpful to know seven routines I do every day to keep myself going and growing.

I created a simple one-page list of those seven steps. Get your copy at   http://thrivedontjustsurvive.com/thrivenow

In addition to that list, I offer a FREE subscription ($97 value) to my newsletter, *THRIVE! Don't Just Survive*

Once or twice each week I share hints as well as frequent gifts to keep you on track in life and How To Thrive! Don't Just Survive

Remember, happiness is your birthright. Take it on!

I deeply appreciate you, my reader. Without you, I cannot make the difference I came here to make for all life and for the planet. If you feel you benefited from this book, I appreciate your leaving me an honest review on my book site and on the site where you purchased my book.

If you see something you do not like, please contact me to see if making a change makes sense to me rather than leave a bad review.

Think about the people you know who may benefit from the information in this book. Send them the link to get their copy and begin their new life now: **http://thrivedontjustsurvive.com**

Thank you in advance for your participation. Together let's change the world one smile at a time.

EXTRA BONUS!!!

I gift you with the song, *THRIVE! Don't Just Survive*

Go here to access your gift:
Recording:
http://thrivedontjustsurvive.com/thrive-song/

lyrics:
http://thrivedontjustsurvive.com/thrive.html

About Ali Bierman

Ali Bierman, known as the Queen of Overcoming, survived two life-altering brain events. Each time the medical community told her to, "Learn to live with it. This is as good as it gets."

Choosing to participate in life rather than watch it go by, Ali seized the opportunity to grow through all the physical and emotional pain it took to create a new life – twice – in her altered brain and altered body.

She lived through a diversity of life experiences as a wife, mom, "professional" volunteer, psychotherapist, artist, composer, musician, specialized kinesiologist, and a metaphysical minister. She produced more than fifty books on topics including parenting, health, relationships, spirituality and her favorite: happiness.

Ali came to the world of specialized kinesiology and metaphysics from a career as a psychotherapist working in crisis care. A very dangerous client cornered and attacked her. The resulting brain injury led to her medical retirement at the age of forty-six. The doctors said she would not heal. Ali did not buy into their paradigm.

More recently she survived surgery to remove a brain tumor that hampered her functioning for three years before its discovery. Losing her ability to talk, to swallow, to walk and do many related tasks allowed her to prove what she says she believes and truly walk her talk.

What few people know about Ali is she was inducted into Psi Chi, The International Honor Society for Psychology, while working on her MA in psychology. You can find her listed in more than one half dozen Who's Who books including Who's Who in

Alternative Medicine. She was also nominated as International Woman of the Year early in her career.

While pursuing her goal of impacting three million lives for the better, she made a good start touching more than 150,000 lives through her writing, teaching, speaking and music, in addition to her private practice.

She lives by the motto, "Be well and happy. In the end, nothing else matters."

Get your FREE gifts and discover more about happiness and health at Ali's sites:

http://thrivedontjustsurvive.com
http://queenofovercoming.com
http://healthyyouuniversity.com
http://metaphysicalministryinternational.com

Follow Ali:

http://facebook.com/thrivedontjustsurvivebyalib
http://www.linkedin.com/in/alibierman
http://www.youtube.com/user/alitlc
https://plus.google.com/+AliBierman/posts
http://pinterest.com/alijbierman/boards/
https://twitter.com/alibierman

If you wish to reach Ali personally for any reason contact her through her website at

http://thrivedontjustsurvive.com/contact

Some Other Books You May Enjoy By Ali Bierman

On Kindle:

Each of these books hit the Top 10 on Amazon Best Seller Lists, most of them hitting #1 in two or more categories for one or more weeks

• What You Don't Know You Don't Know: How Your Brain and Mind Keep You Stuck (#1 Best Seller)
16 months on Best Sellers lists
http://www.amazon.com/ dp/B00QVK41BM

• Mental Illness: Consequences When the Brain Misfires (#1 Best Seller)
http://www.amazon.com/gp/product/B00EPCQ67K/

• Stay At Home Mom: Lousy Pay, Lousy Hours, Priceless Rewards
http://www.amazon.com/gp/product/B00CCYP9O4

• Parents, You Gotta Ask Questions: How To Build Adolescent Self Esteem
http://www.amazon.com/gp/product/B00CD03Y6M/

• How To Repair The Top 7 Relationship Mistakes: Find Romance NOW
http://www.amazon.com/gp/product/B004K6MNXC/

• Cat Lovers: A Story Just For You
http://www.amazon.com/gp/product/B00EPCKSJ2

• Christmas Art To Eat
http://www.amazon.com/dp/B00HGM731O

• Recipes for Living: Fuel for Your Family's Body, Mind and Spirit
http://www.amazon.com/gp/product/B00CD7HRCW

Amazon Paperbacks:

• Stay At Home Mom: Lousy Pay, Lousy Hours, Priceless Rewards
http://www.amazon.com/dp/1453739882

• Romance Killers: Top 7 Mistakes That Doom Relationships
http://www.amazon.com/gp/product/1456320807

• 17 Parenting Mistakes: What To Do Instead
http://www.amazon.com/gp/product/1463762046

• Recipes for Living: Fuel for Your Family's Body, Mind and Spirit
http://www.amazon.com/gp/product/1453739882

Look for these paperback books in 2015:

~ You Can Prevent and Reverse Mental Illness

~ What You Don't Know You Don't Know: How Your Brain and Mind Keep You Stuck

~ Parents, You Gotta Ask Questions: How To Build Adolescent Self Esteem

*To have something you've never had
you must first choose to be someone
you've never been
who does things you've never done.*

Be. Do. Have.

Start healing NOW!

www.ingramcontent.com/pod-product-compliance
Lightning Source LLC
Chambersburg PA
CBHW070804100426
42742CB00012B/2246